Splendors
OF THE
Magnificat

Cover:
The Madonna of the Magnificat *(c. 1481-1485)*
Sandro Botticelli (1445-1510)
Tempera on wood (tondo), diameter: 118 cm (46.4 in.)

Botticelli's refinement and sensitivity reach their full expression in this tondo of the Madonna of the Magnificat. Surrounded by five angels, Mary and the Christ child are closely united, right down to their gestures: Jesus guides his mother's hand as she writes the Magnificat. With their free hands, they together hold a split pomegranate, a symbol of both Mary's fecundity and Christ's passion. The right-hand page of the book contains the first lines of the Magnificat; on the left, the Benedictus, the Canticle of Zechariah, can be discerned. The message of Botticelli's Madonna to the spectator is clear: the Church sings the Benedictus in the morning at the office of Lauds, the Magnificat in the evening at Vespers – meaning that God must be praised ceaselessly, from dawn to dusk, in thanksgiving for sending us his Son.
In a celebration of tota pulchra (total beauty), the artist represents the Virgin as a blond young girl, radiant with beauty, richly dressed and adorned with a veil and translucent ribbons. Descending like beams of blessings, the golden rays of sunlight traverse the star-studded crown, ripple through the Virgin's hair and the angels, embellish their clothing, and extend even to the gilt-edged book.

Publisher: Pierre-Marie Dumont

Editor: Romain Lizé
Art Direction: Elisabeth Hébert

Meditations: Daniel P. Barron, O.M.V.
Presentations of the composers: Richard J. Giarusso
Art commentaries: Emmanuel Bourceret
Translation: John Pepino and Janet Chevrier
Copy editors: Susan Barnes and Andrew Matt
Iconography: Isabelle Mascaras
Production: Annie-Laurie Clément, Sabine Marioni, Marie Cheneval

Acknowledgments: Catherine E. Hubka for her creative assistance with the meditations, and Solange Bosdevesy for her help with the images.

ISBN: 978-0-9798086-6-1
First edition: October 2009

Splendors
of the
Magnificat

Magnificat®

A Celebration of the Magnificat
Romanus Cessario, O.P.

Mary's *Magnificat* geographically places us within the hill country of Judea. The name for this ancient region of the Holy Land comes from a Hebrew word that means "celebrated." So we can discern something of divine providence at work when the Blessed Virgin Mary, immediately after conceiving the Son of God in her womb, hastens to visit her cousin Elizabeth in a place whose name means "celebration." At the home of Zechariah and Elizabeth, in the Judean hills, the world first celebrates the Incarnation of the Son of God.

It comes as no surprise to discover that the biblical text of the *Magnificat*, which is found in the Gospel of St. Luke, ranks among the best known of New Testament verses (Luke 1: 46–55). One indication of the attraction these words exercise on the Christian people appears in the longstanding practice of singing the *Magnificat*. From the earliest days of the Church's formal liturgy, especially in monasteries, Christians have gathered in the evening to sing together the words of Mary's *Magnificat*.

Catholic liturgy both sustains and develops human culture. We see this truth verified especially in the masterpieces of music and art that owe their inspiration to the Christian mysteries. Over the course of the centuries, artists have chosen the mysteries that the *Magnificat* embodies as a theme for their paintings and music. Even in our own day, we find composers setting Mary's *Magnificat* to music. These persons and their musical achievements contribute to fulfilling what the Blessed Virgin herself predicted to her cousin Elizabeth: "From this day all generations will call me blessed."

The present volume by Father Daniel Barron, an Oblate of the Virgin Mary, takes its inspiration from the second nation-wide reunion of the MAGNIFICAT family, the Pilgrimage of Hope held in Boston in 2008. Many persons who attended this two-day retreat gained much spiritual benefit from experiencing the powerful combination of music, sacred artwork, and spiritual commentary that drew upon the *Magnificat*. These pilgrims found their prayer enhanced by hearing what no ear can hear and seeing what no eye can see.

In other words, they found support for their lives of faith.

The *Magnificat* opens up a mystery of divine love that manifests itself in three ways. Each way is represented by a holy person. First, there is the old Jewish woman, Elizabeth, who hears these words sung by a woman, her cousin, pregnant with God's Son. Elizabeth represents the people of Israel, that is, God's chosen people. She stands before Mary as a witness to the fulfillment of God's covenant with Israel. Elizabeth is also with child; she herself embodies a visible sign that God "has remembered his promise of mercy." The name given to this mercy is Jesus Christ. In a broader sense, then, Elizabeth also represents the world and all who inhabit it—that is, each person who has been created for redemption in Christ.

Second, there is Mary herself. The *Magnificat* reveals the unique position that the Mother of the Redeemer enjoys in the Church of her Son. The Christian believer should never forget the divine delicacy at work in the Incarnation of the Son of God. God reverses the natural human expectations of salvation that might favor a vast and rich display of divine power. Instead, God comes among us as a little child. From this moment on, true religion belongs to those who are willing to become like little children. Within the compass of the mystery of her divine maternity, Mary becomes at once mother and highly favored daughter. Thus the greeting of the angel, "Hail, full of grace." So Mary proclaims that God "has looked with favor on his lowly servant." She accepts her littleness.

Third, there is the figure of Everyman. Like everything that is set down in the Sacred Scriptures, the *Magnificat* forms a prayer for all Christian believers. The *Magnificat* belongs on the lips of all those who have been begotten from above by the power of the Holy Spirit and in the waters of Mary's womb—a place that the saints identify as the locale where one is formed into the divine image of Mary's Son. Mary is their spiritual mother, and so Christians pray the *Magnificat*. Even more, they are asked to meditate on the *Magnificat*. They are invited to enter into the rhythms of the *Magnificat* so that their lives will reflect the same attitudes and affections that inform the heart of the Blessed Virgin Mary.

Magnificat in Latin

Magníficat anima mea Dóminum
et exultávit spíritus meus in Deo salutari meo.

Quia respéxit humilitátem ancíllae suae:
ecce enim ex hoc beátam me dicent omnes generationes.

Quia fecit mihi magna qui potens est
et sanctum nomen eius,

Et misericórdia eius a progénie
in progenies timentibus eum.

Fecit poténtiam in brácchio suo:
dispérsit supérbos mente cordis sui.

Depósuit poténtes de sede,
et exaltávit húmiles.

Esuriéntes implévit bonis:
et dívites dimísit inánes,

Suscépit Ísrael, púerum suum,
recordátus misericórdiae suae.

Sicut locútus est ad patres nostros,
Ábraham et sémini eius in sáecula.

Glória Patri, et Filio, et Spiritui Sancto,
sicut erat in princípio, et nunc, et semper,
et in sáecula saeculórum.
Amen.

Magnificat in English

My soul proclaims the greatness of the Lord,
my spirit rejoices in God my Savior
for he has looked with favor on his lowly servant.

From this day all generations will call me blessed:
the Almighty has done great things for me,
and holy is his Name.

He has mercy on those who fear him
in every generation.

He has shown the strength of his arm,
he has scattered the proud in their conceit.

He has cast down the mighty from their thrones,
and has lifted up the lowly.

He has filled the hungry with good things,
and the rich he has sent away empty.

He has come to the help of his servant Israel
for he has remembered his promise of mercy,
the promise he made to our fathers,
to Abraham and his children for ever.

Glory to the Father, and to the Son, and to the Holy Spirit,
as it was in the beginning, is now, and will be for ever.
Amen

Magnificat in English

(Book of Common Prayer, 1662)

My soul doth magnify the Lord
and my spirit hath rejoiced in God my Saviour.
For he hath regarded the lowliness of his handmaiden.

For behold, from henceforth, all generations shall call me blessed.
For he that is mighty hath magnified me
and holy is his Name.

And his mercy is on them that fear him
throughout all generations.

He hath showed strength with his arm
he hath scattered the proud in the imagination of their hearts.

He hath put down the mighty from their seat
and hath exalted the humble and meek.

He hath filled the hungry with good things
and the rich he hath sent empty away.

He remembering his mercy
hath holpen his servant Israel
as he promised to our forefathers,
Abraham and his seed, for ever.

Glory be to the Father, and to the Son, and to the Holy Ghost,
As it was in the beginning, is now, and ever shall be,
world without end.
Amen.

MAGNIFICAT IN GERMAN

(the verses follow Telemann's *Magnificat*)

Meine Seele erhebt den Herrn,
und mein Geist freuet sich Gottes, meines Heilandes,

Denn er hat seine elende Magd angesehen.
Siehe, von nun an werden mich selig preisen alle Kindeskind.

Denn er hat große Ding an mir getan der da mächtig ist
und des Name heilig ist.

Und seine Barmherzigkeit währet immer für und für,
bei denen, die ihn fürchten.

Er übet Gewalt mit seinem Arm,
und zerstreuet, die hoffärtig sind, in ihres Herzens Sinn.
Er stößet, die Gewaltigen vom Stuhl
und erhebt die Niedrigen.

Die Hungrigen füllt er mit Gütern
und läßt die Reichen leer.
Er denket der Barmherzigkeit,
und hilft seinem Diener Israel auf.

Wie er geredt hat unsern Vätern,
Abraham und seinem Samen ewiglich.

Lob und Preis sei Gott dem Vater und dem Sohn
und dem Heiligen Geiste,
wie es war im Anfang, jetzt und immerdar
und von Ewigkeit zu Ewigkeit.
Amen.

Gregorian chant

If legend attributes the authorship of Western plainchant to St. Gregory, history suggests a more complex tale. Gregorian chant is, in fact, the fruit of a constantly evolving and ever growing body of liturgical chants that is first transmitted orally. With the advent of musical notation in 750 A.D., these oral chants begin to be codified in writing. Thus, even though the earliest notated sources date from this period, the chants themselves have been sung by the Church for centuries.

In his famous *Rule*, written in the mid-sixth century, St. Benedict describes the cycle of non-Eucharistic daily prayer known as the Divine Office. Eight services, offered throughout the day, consist mainly of the recitation of psalms, canticles, and antiphons. While certain elements of the Office changed according to the liturgical year, the service of Vespers, offered at dusk, always includes the *Canticle of Mary*, known more commonly as the *Magnificat*. Like the psalmody chanted as part of the Office in numerous monasteries today, the *Magnificat* is often sung in a responsorial fashion, with a solo cantor alternating verses with the choir, as heard here.

While the *Magnificat* is a constant feature of the Vespers service, it is typically preceded and followed by a chant, proper to the day, called an antiphon. The *Magnificat* can be sung to one of eight different melodic formulas known as psalm tones. The tone for a particular day is chosen to match the musical characteristics of the proper antiphon. In the example heard here, the antiphon is that for the service of Vespers for the Feast of the Circumcision, and both the antiphon and the *Magnificat* are sung to the fourth tone *(quarti toni)*.

Rubum quem víderat Móyses
incombústum, conservátam agnóvimus
túam laudábilem virginitátem:
Déi Génitrix, intercéde pro nóbis.

In the bush Moses saw
as burning yet unconsumed,
we recognize the figure
of your admirable virginity.
O Mother of God, intercede for us.

And Mary said:

"My soul magnifies
the Lord..."

The early Christians were known as followers of "The Way." Christians were—and are—pilgrims on a common journey to heaven, our true home. This joyful pilgrimage of faith contains both shadow and light, desolation and consolation. The Virgin Mary herself knew this journey. The Gospel of St. Matthew tells us that Joseph took the child Jesus and his Mother and fled into Egypt. In the Gospel of St. Luke, we read that when Jesus was twelve years old, Joseph and Mary journeyed to Jerusalem, where they lost him and had to search for him anxiously. Also in Luke, we read that Mary undertook a journey of love in haste to the hill country home of Zechariah and Elizabeth. There, the unborn John the Baptist leapt for joy at the presence of Jesus in her womb. There, also, the *Magnificat* was first pronounced in prayer.

And Mary said:
"My soul magnifies the Lord…"

"Magnificat," the Latin first word of Mary's prayer of praise, powerfully connotes Mary's mission—to glorify God. Her very being makes us marvel at the revelation of divine love. God so loved the world that he sent his only Son through her (see John 3: 16; Galatians 4: 4-5).

*One cannot enter the cathedral without being struck by the famous
"Chartres blue" of the 173 windows. They shed a soft half-light, a powerful
invitation to recollection. As one turns to the great western door, the visitor
beholds the immense twelfth-century window dedicated to the childhood and
public life of Christ. It consists of a succession of narrative panels bordered
with floral motifs and fabulous birds. At the bottom center, the Visitation
portrays Elizabeth leaving her house, represented by two pillars, to greet
her cousin who has just arrived. With her left hand raised in a gesture of
greeting, Elizabeth points to the blessed fruit of Mary's womb, whose own
raised hands symbolize the act of thanksgiving that is the Magnificat.*

Through Mary, the Gate of Heaven, the Redeemer came, not to condemn but to open the way for us. In becoming the Mother of God, she became truly the new Eve, the mother of all the living. In spite of the singular graces she received, Mary's heart proclaims the truth that John the Baptist expressed later as the end of his journey approached: "He must increase. I must decrease" (John 3: 30).

As she continues to magnify God from heaven, she tells us what she told the stewards at Cana: "Do whatever he tells you" (John 2: 5). We proclaim the greatness of the Lord on our life pilgrimage whenever we say "yes" to Jesus, who declares "I am the Way" (John 14: 6). We give glory to God when we notice the multitude of ways that He cares for us each day on our journey toward heaven. There are, indeed, dark times when life's journey feels like an aimless wandering in the desert, but at other moments we receive the grace to recognize Jesus' presence with us, as did the two disciples at table with him at Emmaus. We can take courage knowing that Mary understands our plight. Mary, the Star of the Sea, intercedes for us still, and she continues to shine for us like a beacon on our journey homeward.

At left:
Notre Dame Cathedral, Rheims, France *(twelfth century)*

*The north side-aisle sums up at a glance the exceptional character
of the Cathedral of Rheims. The harmony of its proportions, its
slenderness, and its brightness are impressive, and the richness of its
statuary captivates visitors. Indeed, 2,303 sculptures adorn the cathedral,
including those on the interior façade, whose superimposed niches
house Old Testament figures assembled around and above the great
wooden door. In this masterpiece of Gothic art, whose construction
began in 1211 and would last three centuries, nearly all the kings of
France were crowned. The cathedral suffered from German bombing
raids during the First World War, but it was restored thanks to the
invaluable aid of American patrons, the Rockefeller family in particular.*

At right:
Abbey Church of Sainte-Foy, Conques, France
(11th-12th century)

The twenty-first century visitor may think he has been transported back into the Middle Ages when he catches sight of the majestic apse of the abbey church of Sainte-Foy nestled within the hillside village of Conques. The landscape has hardly changed since the mid-eleventh century, when Abbot Odolric undertook the first construction work. A major stop on the road to Santiago de Compostela, this abbey church was intended to house the crowds of pilgrims coming to pray before the relics of Saint Foy, the twelve-year-old girl-martyr of the Roman era. Construction would continue into to the early twelfth century, when the yellow limestone used to build the choir's arches replaced the red sandstone in the lower parts of the apse and chapels. Matching the grey slate of the flagstone roofs, 104 black-and-white stained glass windows, completed in 1994 by the celebrated abstract artist Pierre Soulages, blend discreetly with the spiritual harmony of the Romanesque art.

Next page:
**Cloister of the Monastery of
Santo Domingo de Silos,** Spain
(Late 11th-early 12th century)

In the heart of Castile's ochre land, the visitor discovers one of the most beautiful cloisters handed down to us in the Romanesque style: the monastery of Santo Domingo de Silos. Its architecture, decorations, and bas-reliefs, dating to the turn of the twelfth century, admirably illustrate what beauty meant in the High Middle Ages: the quest for truth and the grace of contemplation. The exuberance of the column capitals and the elegance of their decoration, interwoven with plant arabesques and fantastical animals, revel in subtle and refined artistry. At the cloister's corner piers the Master of Silos has depicted Passion and Resurrection scenes. These masterpieces combine several influences: Byzantine sacrality, Athenian gracefulness, and Roman gravity. A walk in this sacred space is akin to a mystical experience: the visitor becomes a pilgrim on the Gospel road, like these Emmaus pilgrims or the unbelieving Saint Thomas, seeking to recognize Christ in that figure whose gaze is imbued with such goodness.

20

Adrian Willaert
(1490-1562)

In the distinguished company of composers of the early sixteenth century, Adrian Willaert's contemporaries regarded him as the greatest musician of the age. Gioseffo Zarlino, Willaert's one-time pupil and the leading music theorist of the time, referred to his teacher as a "new Pythagoras" whose work offered a summation of all that had come before him.

Born in Flanders, Willaert left home for Paris with the intention of studying law; however, his legal studies were interrupted after an encounter with the composer Jean Mouton, who took him on as a student. After his time in Paris, Willaert, like so many other northern musicians of the time, found work as a musician in Italy, first in service to the d'Este family, and then, beginning in 1527, as chapel master at St. Mark's Basilica in Venice, where he remained until his death in 1562. During his thirty-five year tenure, Willaert oversaw the creation of one of the most impressive musical establishments in Europe, laying the groundwork for the flowering of the high Venetian style under Giovanni Gabrieli and Claudio Monteverdi.

While Willaert's polyphonic Masses tended to be quite elaborate, his *Magnificat* is more functional, avoiding elaborate counterpoint in favor of clarity and simplicity. In this way, Willaert's *Magnificat* is typical of a time when composers focused their energies on Mass settings and motets. In another nod toward tradition, Willaert preserves the practice of responsorial singing associated with the *Magnificat*, alternating portions of polyphony with plainchant. Willaert bases this setting of the *Magnificat* upon the sixth tone *(sexti toni)*, one of eight melodic formulas for psalmody derived from plainchant.

And Mary said:

"My spirit rejoices
in God my Savior…"

I t makes sense to us that Mary would rejoice at the Visitation. What a joy for her to see her barren cousin blessed with child after so many years! What a joy to be welcomed with faith as "the mother of my Lord" (Luke 1: 43). These are the sorts of events we usually think of as causes for rejoicing. These are the sorts of events we would expect to bring Mary joy. *Magnificat* joy, though, is something different, something greater; *Magnificat* joy is characteristic of the one who has heard and believed. When there was no room for them in the inn, Mary remained joyful. She did not lose her joy during the flight into Egypt, nor did she lose it at the prophecy of Simeon. Even at the foot of the Cross, she did not lose her joy in the midst of her deep sufferings. When we find life burdensome and struggle to carry our crosses, Mary invites us to rejoice with her in God the Savior. How can this be?

Pope Benedict XVI has reflected much on this question, and on the erroneous tendency among many to associate Christianity with joylessness, cramped scrupulosity, and narrowness of spirit. He comes to a deceptively simple conclusion about the "cause of our joy." Here is what the Pope says:

> *The root of man's joy is the harmony he enjoys within himself... And only one who can accept himself can also accept the other, can accept the world... If an individual is to accept himself, someone must say to him: "It is good that you exist"—must say it, not with words, but with that act of the entire being that we call love.*

The Cross of Jesus Christ proves that it is good that we exist. In the midst of life's tears, and especially in the face of death, God desires to be with us.

He has purchased us at the price of his own Son's blood. "Love then consists in this, not that we have loved God, but that he has loved us and sent his Son as expiation for our sins… We love because he first loved us" (1 John 4: 10). Since this is God's truth, then we know, as Bishop Sheen would say, "Life is worth living." How can we lose joy when God himself loves us so? "If God is for us, who can be against us?" (Romans 8: 31).

Love is worth the suffering it entails. The "Good News" is not a piece of information, but God's own testimony in the person of his Son and in his Son's mother that God's love always triumphs. Christianity is not about sadness and suffering. God does not delight in punishing us, nor does he ever wish evil upon us. God wills our good and commands us to rejoice! In this light the penances and sufferings embraced by the

Above:
The Census at Bethlehem
Pieter Brueghel the Younger (1564-1638)
After the canvas painted by Pieter Brueghel the Elder (1520/25-1569)
Oil on wood, 120 × 171 cm (47 × 67 in.)

In a Nordic winter landscape, Mary and Joseph reach Bethlehem near the inn that presently serves as a census office. Their arrival goes unnoticed among the people engaged in their daily activities: peasants slaughter a pig; children throw snowballs and slide on the ice; an old woman sweeps snow; men shoulder loads to the market; public officials profit from the census by collecting tithes... Pieter the Younger copied a canvas that his father, Pieter the Elder, painted in 1566—a terrible year for Flanders, suffering from both a severe economic crisis as well as the "Beggar Revolt." The religious drama seems to be enguifed by the mundane scene. Brueghel, however, means to show that the Son of God takes on flesh so as to become like us, a man among men: the Incarnation takes place precisely within the hustle and bustle of history, in the very heart of everyday existence. Mary is thus depicted perched on a donkey with the manger-scene ox nearby to emphasize the humility of the Savior's birth.

Above:
Interior of the Antwerp Cathedral *(1609)*
Hendrik van Steenwijk (1580-1649) and Jan Brueghel the Elder,
also known as "Velvet" Brueghel (1568-1625)
Oil on canvas, 45.2 × 62.5 cm (18 × 25 in.)

*Hendrik van Steenwijk, a specialist in church interiors, collaborated on this 1609
canvas with Jan "Velvet" Brueghel who painted the figures. Beyond its decorative
features, the historical and sociological witness is particulary striking. Thus, the 1596
rood-screen and the guilds' altars with their wooden enclosures have long since
disappeared. Each detail faithfully reproduces the attitudes of the faithful
of that time, in an open space with neither pew nor chair. Flemish ladies wear their
peculiar pointy-hooded cloaks, dogs gambol about freely, gentlemen bear swords
at their sides, beggars with children seek alms, while figures in the nave attend
Mass on their knees... The house of God is also a house that embraces all people.*

saints must not be dismissed as masochistic excesses, but rather pondered as wild expressions of hearts in love with God.

And so indeed, Mary would pray the *Magnificat* at the foot of the Cross. And a new joy appears! When Jesus says, "Woman, behold your son" (John 19: 26), the Mother of God accepts us as her own. Her mother's heart understands the secret of love. The labor pains she endured for the birth of the Church she easily forgot in light of our salvation. Mary continues to take our tears and turn them into smiles. St. Louis de Montfort writes: "Happy, a thousand times happy, is the soul here below to whom the Holy Spirit reveals the secret of Mary…"

Giovanni Gabrieli
(1557-1612)

In sixteenth-century Venice, religious and civic life overlapped freely, and music at St. Mark's Basilica served the liturgy of the Church while celebrating the grandeur and authority of the state. In this context, the music program at St. Mark's grew throughout the century to become one of the most impressive in all Europe. When Giovanni Gabrieli was hired as second organist in 1585, the preeminence of St. Mark's in the European musical landscape was assured. Inspired by the finest singers and instrumentalists available, Gabrieli wrote music of unprecedented opulence to the honor of God and the glory of Venice.

By the 1580s, polychoral music (written for two or more distinct groups of singers) had already enjoyed a distinguished history in northern Italy, above all in Venice. In the simplest polychoral works, different choirs, often situated far apart from each other, would sing alternate portions of a piece in a kind of musical dialogue. One can well imagine the stunning, multi-dimensional effect of such music in a space as expansive as St. Mark's. For centuries, chanted psalms and canticles had been performed in a similar fashion, with groups of singers alternating verses on opposite sides of the chancel. Thus, a polychoral setting of the *Magnificat*, even one as grand as the version for twelve voices heard here, was a natural extension of an ancient liturgical practice.

In Gabrieli's polychoral works, his bold juxtaposition of voices creates a sonority of unprecedented variety, and the fluid rhythms of so much sixteenth-century polyphony are replaced by short, declamatory phrases bursting with energy. At St. Mark's, instruments, doubling the voice parts, would have added to the splendor of the polychoral texture.

And Mary said:

"HE HAS LOOKED WITH FAVOR ON HIS LOWLY SERVANT."

Previous page:
The Pietà *(1498-1499)*
Michelangelo Buonarroti (1475-1564)
The band bears the signature:
"MICHEL. ANGELUS. BONAROTUS. FLORENT. FACIEBAT"
Marble sculpture, height: 174 cm (68.5 in.)
St. Peter's Basilica, Rome, Vatican City

*Michelangelo was twenty-three when Cardinal Jean Bilhères de Lagraulas, French
ambassador to the pope, commissioned him to produce a Pietà in 1498. One year later,
the young artist presented his masterpiece, hewn from a single block of Carrara marble.
Unlike the desolation customary in the Pietà genre, Michelangelo's work reveals the
tranquil face of a Virgin adorned with eternal youth. She seems to be of the same age as
the Son on her lap. Her face is bowed in an attitude of profound recollection and humble
submission to the divine will. Her serene countenance is in stark contrast to the rippling
drapery, itself the work of a virtuoso. The Virgin's dress is ornamented with a ribbon
that bears Michelangelo's name. Never again would his signature appear on a work.*

onfronted with our
sinfulness, we want to
hide from God. Like
Adam and Eve ashamed of
their nakedness, or the elder
son embittered at his prodigal brother's return, we shrink
from the gaze of divine love.
As nocturnal creatures crawl
into the shadows, so we avoid
the intense rays of the Son. We
recoil from what we most need
and desire. This paradox points
us to Mary, the woman who
dared to return the look.

The Lord's look, however,
is not the scowl of an angry
judge. God's experience of
Mary's immaculate beauty
mirrors Adam's astonish-
ment as he encounters the
first woman: "This one at last
is bone of my bone and flesh
of my flesh!" (Genesis 2: 23).
The theologian Hans Urs von
Balthasar reflects deeply on
the wonder of this first meeting of man and woman created
in God's image. The man, he
says, is like a word *(Wort)*
cried out by God, and the
woman is the answer *(Antwort)*.
Man is the "face," while
woman is the "look" in return.

This fundamental anthropology shapes von Balthasar's understanding of Jesus Christ as the Word made flesh, and his insight that the face of Christ is the quintessence of beauty. In his theology, Mary's response becomes the archetype of our "look" toward God. He often quotes the poet Paul Claudel, who puts it this way:

> *What will be the power of her face? Or of a direct glance from her eyes, those eyes that disturbed the Trinity itself, and invited it to create the world? What will be the power of that mouth which, when it opened to say Yes, robbed the Word of the power to breathe?*

As man and woman stand "face to face," so does the human person long to behold God face to face. Moses said, "Do let me see your glory!" but he was not allowed to see God's face, for "no man sees me and lives" (Exodus 33: 18-20). The Psalms frequently express our ache to see God: "Athirst is my soul for the living God. When shall I behold him face to face?" (Psalm 42: 2). St. Paul points to this desire when he says "Eye has not seen... nor has it dawned on man what God has prepared for those who love him" (1 Corinthians 2: 9). Later in the same epistle, he says, "Now we see as in a mirror dimly, but then face to face... At present I know partially, then I shall know even as I am known" (1 Corinthians 13: 12).

Whether we have strayed like the prodigal son or served with resentment like the elder, Mary coaxes us out of the shadows and begs us to join the feast.

Above:
**View of the San Marco Canal and San Giorgio Maggiore Island,
with the Church of San Giorgio Maggiore,** Venice, Italy
Begun by Andrea Palladio in 1566, completed by Vicenzo Scamozzi in 1610.

*An ideal harmony suffuses this view of San Giorgio Maggiore Island. The church
seems to float on Venice's lagoon while the rays of the setting sun accentuate the
façade's immaculate marble and the rose and white campanile. Such an effect
does not come as a lucky stroke of nature; rather it was willed by one of the
greatest architects of the Renaissance. Indeed Andrea Palladio always designed
his constructions so as to complement their locale, atmosphere, and landscape.
Begun in 1566, the white façade of San Giorgio Maggiore presents a typically
Palladian composition: two classical façades seem to overlap thanks to the
pediment and the four monumental columns that create a second spatial plane in
the foreground, resulting in two harmonic systems of architectural counterpoint.*

Previous page:
The Visitation
Paolo Caliari called Veronese (1528-1588)
Oil on canvas

*This scene is viewed from below, a clue that the painting was intended for a ceiling.
Because of this perspective, the image takes on a majestic grandeur typical of the Venetian
painter Veronese. His perspectives are often bold and his compositions are marked by
the rhythm of trompe-l'œil colonnades. Emblematic of Veronese's dramatic style are
his dizzying treatment of fabrics and a fondness for inscribing the interplay of lines within
a triangular configuration. With a gesture at once intimate and respectful, Elizabeth greets
her cousin Mary with a reverent bow. To the right, Zechariah's body is poised in a blend
of amazement and expectation that draws the viewer to share in his heightened sense of awe.*

Standing in solidarity with our lowliness, she praises the Father for his prodigality. As the father in the parable assured the elder son, "Everything I have is yours" (Luke 15: 31), our Father did not withhold from us even his only Son. We rejoice with Mary that he has looked upon his lowly servants. We rejoice that Jesus does far more than kill the fattened calf for us; he stoops to wash our feet.

Whoever wishes to be great among
you shall be your servant;
whoever wishes to be first among
you shall be your slave.
Just so, the Son of Man did not
come to be served
but to serve ...
Matthew 20: 26-28

Orlando Gibbons
(1583-1625)

Few English composers of the early seventeenth-century were held in higher esteem than Orlando Gibbons. Organist of the Chapel Royal and, subsequently, of Westminster Abbey, Gibbons was such a skillful keyboard player that the Dean of Westminster dubbed him the "best" of his age—no small compliment, since Gibbons's contemporaries included the likes of William Byrd, Thomas Tomkins, and Thomas Weelkes. Though his output is relatively modest, his contributions to the repertoire of Anglican anthems and service music have become hallmarks of the venerable English choral tradition.

With the Acts of Supremacy and Union, passed by Elizabeth I in 1559, the Roman Catholic offices of Vespers and Compline were conflated into a new, distinctly Anglican service known as Evensong. The *Magnificat* and the *Nunc Dimittis* were codified as elements of the Evensong liturgy, and it was for this new context that Gibbons composed his *Magnificat*. As part of a "short service," the setting of the *Magnificat* would have been paired with a setting of the *Nunc Dimittis*.

While Anglican practice favored a simpler style of music, the importance of music as a fundamental part of the liturgy was upheld. As stated in the Injunctions of 1559, sacred music was to be "modest" and "plainly understood." In its succinct, syllabic style and its use of the vernacular, Gibbons's *Magnificat* is very much a product of its time and a classic example of the style of the "short service." More elaborate and expansive settings of the Evensong canticles were known as "great services," the most famous of which was written by William Byrd.

And Mary said:

"All generations
will call me blessed…"

Rubens painted this Visitation as a deliciously intimate scene: Mary, with her arched back, is visibly pregnant under her rose- and blue-colored dress. Wearing a broad-brimmed Flemish hat, she leans on the banister with her right hand. With the other hand she raises her red cape slightly so as to reveal to her cousin Elizabeth the Child whom she bears in her womb. For her part, Elizabeth's index finger lightly grazes her cousin's belly in a silent gesture that eloquently foreshadows her own son John the Baptist's full-throated prophecy as he points to Jesus at the Jordan: Ecce Agnus Dei ("Behold the Lamb of God" [Jn. 1: 29]). In the middle distance the two husbands, Joseph and Zechariah, converse together. To the left, a barely visible maid carrying a laundry basket watches the viewer. The viewer, in turn, feels called upon as a witness by this gaze and thereby becomes involved in the scene taking place just above him, on the steps of an ancient palace. In his choice of colors and composition, Rubens has obviously drawn his inspiration from the Venetian painters. He had been back from Italy three years when the harquebusiers' guild commissioned a triptych from him in 1610 to adorn their chapel in the cathedral of Antwerp [an "harquebusier" is a soldier whose weapon, the harquebus or hackbut, is an earlier version of the musket]. Rubens's magnificent triptych depicts the Descent from the Cross, framed on the left by this Visitation and on the right by the Presentation in the Temple.

With simple and profound humility the Virgin Mary pronounces this statement about herself. The humility that made her shrink from the angel's greeting is the same humility with which she now proclaims her role in God's plan of redemption. As a daughter of the covenant, how she must have longed to hear that the coming of the Messiah was near! Now, with the Incarnation resting within her, Mary proclaims to Elizabeth that all generations will indeed call her "blessed." Her humility allows her to acknowledge what the Almighty has done for her. Deep in her heart, she grasps the profound mystery unfolding within her.

Mary's prophecy has proved true. All generations of believers have honored her and have sung her words in the *Magnificat*. Her praises are sung on every continent and in nearly every known language. The Virgin Mary's "yes" was the beginning of God's fulfillment of his own plan to redeem man. She is "blessed" because, in the purity of her heart that no sin ever touched, nor disordered attachment tainted, she gave herself entirely to God's plan. What gratitude and love flow from Mary's blessedness! Her charity and beauty shine from the face of the Lord Jesus as he proclaims the eight Beatitudes (see Matthew 5: 3-10).

At right:
The Nave of Westminster Abbey (1245-1376), London, England

The venue for the coronation and burial of most of the kings and queens of England, Westminster Abbey, a stone's throw from Big Ben, is the most famous church in London. Its name, from the Old French Ouestmoutiers or "Western Abbey," derives from the Benedictine monastery, founded in the tenth century by Saint Dunstan, which is located to the west of the city. In the eleventh century King Edward the Confessor established a collegiate church there dedicated to Saint Peter where William I (the Conqueror) would soon be crowned King of England in 1066. In 1245 King Henry III chose to give a beautiful setting to Edward the Confessor's grave and thus rebuilt the existing church in the Gothic style. In 1376, architect Henry Yevele entirely recast the nave as we see it today. Among the Westminster organists, the most famous is probably the composer Orlando Gibbons, who conducted the music for James I's funeral in 1625.

Blessed among women is Mary, poor in spirit, Mother of Sorrows, meek and merciful, athirst for righteousness, clean of heart, Queen of Peace, and Queen of Martyrs.

In her son's Beatitudes, we find a path to holiness in our own generation. They capture the interior dispositions necessary for our own *fiat*. The beauty of Mary's "yes" is its unconditional, perfect receptivity. St. Thomas of Villanova exclaims: "O powerful *Fiat*! For with a *fiat* God created light, heaven, earth; but with Mary's *fiat*, God became man." By her willingness to receive God completely, she performed a work more fruitful than any labor in history. Too often Pelagian attitudes cling to us like cockleburs. We assent to the gratuitousness of grace, but live under unspoken pressures to perform great acts in order to be saved. The key to "saving your soul" is not keeping the rules, but receiving God. Jesus himself confirms this in his reply to the woman who cried out, "Blessed is the womb that carried you and the breasts at which you nursed." He replied, "Rather, blessed are those who hear the word of God and observe it" (Luke 11: 27-28).

Right page:
Music score for alto and bass from Magnificat for four voices
by Flemish composer Cornelis Verdonck (1563-1625), painting by Martin de Vos (1532-1603)

This is our vocation. We, in turn, are called
to pronounce that same *fiat*, to receive the
Word and let it bear fruit in love. In communion with the saints of all generations, we
receive God's invitation to say "yes," and to
be "blessed." Mary, for her part, stands ready
to help us receive the Lord. St. Lawrence of
Brindisi puts it this way:

> *God wants everyone, everyone, to learn this truth
> from childhood on: that he who trusts in Mary, that
> he who relies on Mary, will never be abandoned, either
> in this world or in the next.*

Tomás Torrejón y Velasco
(1644-1728)

Portrait of García Hurtado de Mendoza, viceroy of Peru (1590-1596)

The Spanish composer Tomás Torrejón y Velasco was born near Madrid in 1644. At the age of fourteen, he entered service as a page in the household of the Count of Lemos, who was appointed viceroy of Peru in 1667. Leaving Spain for his new post, the Count took with him over one hundred personal attendants, including his young page Tomás. In the New World, Torrejón y Velasco served as a military and judicial official before being appointed chapel master of Lima Cathedral in 1676, where he remained until his death in 1728. Little is known of the composer's early training, but the variety of tasks assigned to him in Lima suggests a particularly wide-ranging educational background.

As a composer, Torrejón y Velasco was especially renowned for his *villancicos*, a uniquely Spanish genre with its roots in fifteenth-century popular song. Beginning in the second half of the sixteenth century, the form of the *villancico* was gradually adapted to religious use, finding a place in the liturgy on high feast days. Though the texts (sung in the vernacular) were of a devotional nature, the genre's secular origins were retained with dance-like rhythms and simple, tuneful melodies. By the seventeenth century, the *villancico* had almost completely supplanted the Latin motet in Spanish sacred music, and Torrejón y Velasco was acknowledged throughout the New World as a master of the genre. Even in a work like the *Magnificat* heard here, the lively rhythms and syllabic declamation testify to the pervasive influence of the *villancico* style. Among other accomplishments, Torrejón y Velasco is remembered as the composer of the earliest surviving opera (*La purpúra de la rosa*, 1701) written in the New World.

And Mary said:

"THE ALMIGHTY HAS DONE GREAT THINGS FOR ME..."

Previous page:
Our Lady of Guadalupe
(eighteenth century)

This depiction of the Virgin, an eighteenth-century anonymous work, is a faithful adaptation of the miraculous image preserved in the Basilica of Our Lady of Guadalupe. The Basilica was built on the site north of Mexico City where, on December 9, 1531, the Virgin appeared on Mount Tepeyac with the radiant features of a young olive-skinned woman. She appeared to Juan Diego, a recently baptized Aztec peasant widower, asking him to go to the bishop of Mexico and to request in her name that a shrine be built at Tepeyac, where she promised to pour out her grace upon those who invoked her. The prelate, disbelieving at first, asked the seer for a sign from the Virgin. On December 12, during her fourth and last apparition to Juan Diego, Mary sent him to gather roses on the hilltop. Juan Diego, dumbfounded at such an abundance of roses blooming in the middle of winter, filled his tilma—the traditional Aztec cloak— with fresh flowers. Upon arriving at the bishop's palace he opened his tilma in the presence of the bishop and his court. All were astounded to find the Virgin's image imprinted on the cloak. The miraculous image shows a woman with native features and dress. She is supported by an angel whose wings are reminiscent of one of the major gods of the traditional religion of that area. Echoing the text of the Apocalypse, she appears to be "clothed with the sun, with the moon under her feet" (Revelation 12: 1), while gold stars cover her blue mantle. The black girdle about her waist signifies that she is pregnant. Thus, the image beautifully depicts how Christ is to be «born» again among the peoples of the New World. The Virgin of Guadalupe has since become the object of immense veneration in Mexico and throughout the Americas; she was proclaimed Patroness of Mexico in 1737, and Patroness of the Americas in 1945 by Pope Pius XII.

At right:
Cathedral of Our Lady of the Immaculate Conception *(1540-1704)*
Campeche, Mexico

The glowing white façade of Campeche Cathedral is outlined against the ultramarine sky of the Yucatán Peninsula. This sober, baroque edifice, with its crown-shaped bell towers, stands where the conquistador Francisco de Montejo in 1540 first built a lime-and-pebble, thatch-roofed chapel, the first church in Yucatán. Not until 1704 was the cathedral completed, at the same time as the ramparts intended to protect the town from marauders. The bustling port of Campeche exported cargoes of wood, tobacco, pepper, vanilla, chewing gum, and incense, which were such an incitement to greed that the town was pillaged on numerous occasions in the seventeenth century. An underground passageway was even added, leading from beneath the altar to the garrison's fort, so that clergy could escape from pirates who relentlessly sacked the cathedral for its gold decorations.

The book of Proverbs concludes with the words of King Lemuel of Massa recounting the advice of his mother. She warns him of the dangers of women and of drinking. Many a man has met his downfall, she intimates, by surrendering his vigor to a woman. She goes on to extol the virtues of a worthy wife.

When one finds a worthy wife,
her value is far beyond pearls.
Her husband, entrusting his heart
to her, has an unfailing prize.
She brings him good, and not evil,
all the days of her life…
She reaches out her hands
to the poor, and extends
her arms to the needy…
She is clothed with strength
and dignity, and she laughs
at the days to come.
She opens her mouth in wisdom, and
on her tongue is kindly counsel…
Her children rise up and praise her;
her husband, too, extols her:
"Many are the women of proven
worth, but you have excelled them
all."

Proverbs 31: 10-12, 20,
25-26, 28-29

Certainly the Scriptures portray many great women who met King Lemuel's criteria: Sarah, Rachel, Esther, Judith, and Ruth. What can we say, however, about

Mary, the woman known as the Spouse of the Holy Spirit? She has excelled them all. God literally placed himself in her hands. He entrusted his heart to her, and he treasures her as an unfailing prize. The Fathers of the Church identify her as the Woman who crushed the head of the serpent (see Genesis 3: 15), and the Bride, the Woman clothed with the sun (Revelation 12: 1).

Above:
Angels overhanging the altarpiece of St. Joseph's chapel, St. Francis Xavier Church
(eighteenth century)
Tepotzotlán, Mexico
Painted and gilded wood, 133 × 100 cm (52 × 33 in.)

These two polychrome and gilded wood angels hover in dazzling expectation over the altarpiece of Saint Joseph's chapel, in St. Francis Xavier Church. Their resplendent clothing reflects in miniature the shimmering vitality of the church as a whole, a masterpiece of Churrigueresque architecture. The term designates late baroque art in Spain, Mexico, and South America. Derived from the name of a family of Spanish architects and sculptors, the Churrigueras, this style is characterized by a profusion of sculptures decorated in gold leaf and lively colors, completely covering the walls from floor to ceiling.

In her lowliness, the Virgin Mary wants all generations to know that her blessedness comes not from great things she has done, but from those the Almighty has done for her. Mary's song is certainly one of gratitude and praise. Her *Magnificat* betrays more than just awareness that she is the privileged one who will bring forth Israel's Messiah. There is something more seminal, more personal. Veiled behind her words is a glimpse of her interior life, her relationship with the Lord. We can imagine the tenderness in her voice as she recounted the Lord's mighty deeds. Mary seems to sense somehow the marvel of her sinless conception in the womb of St. Anne. What greater grace could we imagine than for the Mother of the Redeemer to share in the fruits of redemption while she was herself unborn? Who could ever fathom the richness of her relationship with the Trinity? The limits of language leave us mute before this ineffable union.

Neither prophets nor poets, neither sages nor scholars could ever exhaust the mystery of Mary. *De Maria numquam satis*, as St. Bernard put it: "Concerning Mary, one can never say enough." Her visage continues to inspire artists and composers, preachers, and theologians. Still, by her uniquely graceful instruction, she always redirects our eyes toward the Lord. Without our ever realizing it, our admiration for her is transformed, and we adore her Lord. For Mary, the Almighty alone is great, and he does great things for all those who let him.

At left:
Sagrario Metropolitano Church (1749-1768), Mexico City, Mexico

The parish church of Sagrario Metropolitano, adjacent to the cathedral of Mexico, is one of the most beautiful examples of Churrigueresque baroque. Construction began in 1749 following the blueprints of Lorenzo Rodríguez, and the church was consecrated in 1768. Typical Churrigueresque columns lend rhythm to the two-story façade. Known as estípites (in botany, this term signifies woody palm stems), these flamboyantly decorated columns are punctuated with square sections and divided by horizontal moldings. Narrower at their base than at their top, they draw one's gaze heavenward. Crowning the intricate façade, a cornice adorned with finely carved statuettes stands out in dramatic chiaroscuro against the sky.

Marc-Antoine Charpentier
(1643-1704)

To make one's living as a composer at any time is hard work, but it was an especially onerous task in late seventeenth-century France. Jean-Baptiste Lully (1632-1687), court composer to Louis XIV, and one of the most unscrupulous, power-hungry musicians imaginable, used his influence to assume almost absolute control over the French musical establishment. As a composer, Marc-Antoine Charpentier was surely the equal of Lully, but in spite of his talents, politics kept him from securing a coveted position at the court of the Sun King.

After study in Rome in the 1660s, Charpentier returned to Paris, where he worked diligently to build his reputation as a composer in this challenging environment. Early in the 1670s, he had the good fortune of meeting the playwright Molière, who engaged him to write music for his theater troupe. Throughout his career, Charpentier also maintained a close connection with the Jesuits, eventually winning the job of music director at St. Louis Church, the main Jesuit church in Paris. Outside of an appointment at court, Charpentier's post at St. Louis was one of the most desirable in French musical life.

Charpentier's association with the Jesuits explains his strong focus on sacred music. Among Charpentier's sacred works, pieces on Marian themes are especially prevalent, and the *Magnificat* heard here is one of his ten settings of this text. Written for voices and continuo, this setting of the *Magnificat* is decidedly understated, especially when compared with his more lavish versions. As a result, this *Magnificat* captures something of the intimacy and humility of Mary's song of praise.

And Mary said:

"HOLY IS HIS NAME."

Previous page:
The Magnificat Madonna
Jean-Baptiste Jouvenet (1644-1717)
Oil on canvas

*In this scene of the Visitation, Jean-Baptiste Jouvenet has painted the precise
moment when Mary utters the Magnificat. The Virgin, with outstretched arms and
raised eyes, sing the wonders of the Lord. Her whole being is in rapture, to such
a degree that the figures around her seem to feel the overwhelming effects of her
experience: Elizabeth bows in reverence before her Savior's mother; Joseph steadies
a staggering donkey, and even the fabrics rustle and roil with awe. Jean-Baptiste
Jouvenet, a disciple of Charles Le Brun, was a classical painter with a baroque flair
and an ardent colorist. Considered an excellent draftsman by his contemporaries,
he began painting with his left hand after a stroke left his right hand paralyzed.*

The names of the great rulers of history evoke powerful images of colorful personages. Depending on your origins and beliefs, their names may arouse quite different emotions. A name revealed, regardless of the person's virtue, implies a connection. When we share our name, we invite the other into the experience of knowing us. In a very real way, a name is the sacrament of the person. God revealed his name, the sacrament of his Person, through the burning bush: "I AM who I AM" (Exodus 3: 14). In the Decalogue, honoring this name is second only to worshipping God exclusively. Through his name, God made himself personally available to the world and vulnerable to the blasphemies of those who would reject him. God, it seems, would rather be cursed than unknown.

When God became incarnate, his vulnerability reached the extreme. "He came unto his own, but his own did not accept him" (John 1: 11). He did not come with a heart of stone, but "meek and humble of heart," ready to be wounded (Matthew 11: 29). Because Judas was one of the Lord's chosen apostles, his kiss pained Jesus far more than the scourging (see Luke 22: 48).

At left:
***Louis XIV, King of France** (1701)*
Hyacinthe Rigaud (1659-1743)
Oil on canvas, 277 × 194 cm (109 × 76.4 in.)

*Louis XIV poses in the full splendor of his majesty. The king is portrayed at sixty-three years
of age in coronation attire, his sword within easy grasp and his right hand resting casually
on his scepter. Each carefully staged detail lends calculated force to this nonchalant depiction
of the quintessence of absolute power: the choreographed carelessness; the gargantuan cloak
cast effortlessly over his shoulder; the incipient dance step; the upside-down scepter, and
the crown resting harmlessly upon a stool. In this regal composition Hyacinthe Rigaud has
updated the official court portrait by adding a specifically French sort of elegance, halfway
between classical severity and baroque exuberance. Though the figure is solemn, the textile
components swirl in eddies of extravagance. This painting was commissioned as a gift for
his grandson, the king of Spain, Philip V. It so pleased Louis XIV, however, that he kept
it for himself, had a copy made in its stead, and dispatched the duplicate to Madrid.*

St. Paul describes Christ's *kenosis* this way:

He emptied himself, taking the form of a slave, coming in human likeness; and found human in appearance, he humbled himself, becoming obedient to death, even death on a cross. Because of this, God greatly exalted him and bestowed on him the name that is above every name…

Philippians 2: 7-9

Jesus became a slave because he wanted to call us friends who know what the Master is about, and who make requests of the Father in his name (see John 15: 16). Jesus came to show us the Father and taught us to pray "hallowed be thy name" (see John 14: 8; Matthew 6: 9).

In the fulness of time, God sent the angel Gabriel to a virgin of Nazareth, "and the virgin's name was Mary" (Luke 1: 27).

Above:
Château of Versailles (1661-1682), France
West façade viewed from the Park

Nothing exemplifies French classicism better than this harmonious prospect of the
château of Versailles. Built by the architects le Vau and Mansart between 1661 and
1682, the immense, 570 meter-long (623 yds) west façade is reflected in the pool at
the feet of Marie Antoinette's apartments and the Mirror Gallery. The Rhône, by
sculptor Jean-Baptiste Tuby, reclines in the foreground. It is one of the eight bronze
sculptures of the rivers and streams of France that decorate the reflecting pond, which
was excavated in 1684. In this alliance of stone, sky, and water resides one of the most
essential aspects of the French spirit that reached its acme in this château and its
park, both products of Louis XIV's will and thought. Water, symbol (here) of life's
ephemeral passions, evokes in its reflection the fragility of this world that appears so
solid and orderly on the surface, all the while referring back to God's merciful gaze
upon mankind. Hungry for pleasures and surprises as well as for mysticism, the Grand
Siècle bore witness to a religious yearning that strove with all its might to reconcile
worldly glory with the glory made manifest on the Cross and in the Resurrection.

67

The angel announced that she would bear a son, and "name him Jesus" (Luke 1: 31). Without Mary, in other words, the Word neither becomes flesh nor receives his name. In her name, we receive the name by which we are saved. Many children learn their first prayers on the laps of their mothers. Perhaps the Lord's Prayer was inspired by his mother's: "Holy is his name."

God says to us, as to Mary, "Fear not… I have called you by name: you are mine" (Isaiah 43: 1). He wants to know us and to be known by us, making our hearts like his:

> I will prove the holiness of my great name, profaned among the nations, in whose midst you have profaned it. Thus the nations shall know that I am the LORD, says the Lord GOD, when in their sight I prove my holiness through you… I will give you a new heart and place a new spirit within you, taking from your bodies your stony hearts and giving you natural hearts. I will put my spirit within you and make you live by my statutes, careful to observe my decrees. You shall live in the land I gave your fathers; you shall be my people, and I will be your God.
>
> Ezekiel 36: 23-28

At left:
The Assumption of the Virgin (1656)
Philippe de Champaigne (1602-1674)
Oil on canvas (tondo), diameter: 193 cm (76 in.)

Philippe de Champaigne is well known for the vividness of his colors, particularly for this blue, which is an invitation to contemplative calm. Except for the Virgin's rose dress, blue is the dominant color, enlivened by the drapery and by the effervescence of the cherubs (putti) flitting about—even within the folds of Mary's mantle. Champaigne, an essentially religious painter with Jansenist leanings, is the perfect representative of French classicism. The primary intention of his paintings is to lift the faithful to prayer and to spiritual exercises. Such heartfelt Christian sentiment permeates this Assumption, which was commissioned by the Queen of France, Anne of Austria, to adorn the Val-de-Grâce convent in Paris.

Georg Philipp Telemann
(1681-1767)

In 1722, the Leipzig town council voted unanimously to hire Georg Philipp Telemann as the new cantor of the St. Thomas Church, one of the most prestigious musical posts in Germany. Telemann, then director of church music in Hamburg, declined the offer. Eventually, the council engaged a then less renowned musician by the name of Johann Sebastian Bach. As suggested by this account, Telemann was regarded by his contemporaries as one of the greatest composers of the day. With over 3000 works spanning all genres and a reputation that extended across Europe, Telemann was the model of a professional composer. However, after his death, interest in Telemann's music declined dramatically and remained low throughout the next two centuries. Only very recently has Telemann's music begun to receive again the attention that it merits.

In Lutheran Germany, the Office of Vespers was restructured as an afternoon service on Saturdays, Sundays, and feast days. Like its pre-Reformation ancestor, the Lutheran Vespers liturgy included psalms, readings, hymns, and the *Magnificat*. The musical settings for Vespers were often quite simple, with unison melodies sung in German by the congregation. On feast days, portions of the service (sometimes set in Latin), were presented in more elaborate settings like the one heard here. Scholars do not know precisely when Telemann wrote his German *Magnificat*, but it dates possibly from his years in Hamburg (1721-1767) when, as director of music for the city's five main churches, he was required to compose vast quantities of sacred music. The seven movements of Telemann's *Magnificat* alternate between choral and solo singing and feature dramatic examples of text painting common to much Lutheran church music.

And Mary said:

"HE HAS MERCY ON THOSE WHO FEAR HIM IN EVERY GENERATION."

Mercy: love in the face of weakness. Man, without God, shows himself utterly weak. In spite of our cleverest efforts to mask this reality—even from ourselves—myriads of fears rule our weak and sinful hearts. Some of us fear, above all else, the bruising of our pride. Others fear being forgotten, or overlooked, or unappreciated. Still others fear physical illness, or financial ruin, or the loss of treasured possessions. Still others fear whatever they cannot figure out, whatever challenges their sense of intellectual control. Many of us may have indeed earned our fears, but who of us, alone, has any strength to face them?

C. S. Lewis reflected on his own fears in *The Four Loves*. He warns that those who want to be safe from fear and pain risk living without love:

There is no safe investment. To love at all is to be vulnerable. Love anything, and your heart will certainly be wrung and possibly be broken. If you want to make sure of keeping it intact, you must give your heart to no one, not even to an animal. Wrap it carefully round with hobbies and little luxuries; avoid all entanglements; lock it up safe in the casket or coffin of your selfishness. But in that casket—safe, dark, motionless, airless—it will change. It will not be broken; it will become unbreakable, impenetrable, irredeemable... The only place outside Heaven where you can be perfectly safe from all the dangers and perturbations of love is Hell.

From this perspective we can begin to understand St. Paul's paradoxical teaching: "When I am weak, it is then that I am strong" (2 Corinthians 12: 10).

St. Paul refers not to moral or physical weakness, but to the brokenness and vulnerability that mark the human condition. This weakness makes one capable of giving and receiving love. St. Thérèse of the Child Jesus would call such weakness "littleness." She thus exclaimed, "I rejoice to be little, for only children and those who are like them will enter the kingdom of heaven!" As the Preface for the Martyrs puts it, "You choose the weak and make them strong in bearing witness you." Mary understood her weakness, but she also understood God's mercy. She accepted the angel's reassuring words: "Do not be afraid" (Luke 1: 30).

God has mercy on those who fear him. God's heart always responds to us—all our fears and weakness and misery—with love. Jesus' heart was moved with pity—even pierced with a lance for love of us. On the night before he died, he promised not to leave us orphans. His perfect love, the Holy Spirit, casts out our fears, and transforms our weakness into fear of the Lord. Mary testifies that, in our profound weakness, we need only turn to the Father of mercies, to our Father who is "slow to anger, and abounding in kindness" (Psalm 103: 8). And when we do, we learn—perhaps to our astonishment—that fear of the Lord is nothing else than the dread of ever being separated from such Love.

Above:
Two Angels *(1745)*
Polychrome and gilded wood sculpture
St. Martin's Church, Orignac, France

These two charming cherubs, in eighteenth-century polychrome and gilded wood,
decorate the pedestal of the Pietà in the parish church of Orignac, in the French upper
Pyrenees. This region is home to a surprising number of baroque altarpieces. Though
its churches are very plain on the outside, they offer quite magnificent decors once
one crosses their threshold. The devotion and generosity of the people and the artistry
of four successive generations of a dynasty of baroque sculptors, the Ferrère family,
from the village of Asté were responsible for this magnificence. In its workshops this
family built most of the altarpieces in the upper Pyrenees between 1620 and 1795.
No fewer than fifty-nine churches were decorated in this style: twisted columns,
cherubs, decorative motifs—all sculpted in wood and gilded with fine gold.

Previous page:
The Assumption of Mary *(1727)*
Carlo Carlone (1686-1775)
Draft for the fresco in the transept of the parish church of Groß-Siegharts, Austria
Oil on canvas, 119 × 112 cm (47 × 44 in.)

The artist of this Assumption, Carlo Carlone, is one of the Northern Italian artists who
distinguished themselves with their rococo style in central Europe during the eighteenth
century. Attracted by construction sites whose size was unheard of in Italy, he responded
to the invitation of princes eager to assert their authority by means of artistic opulence.
Carlone thus spent the best years of his career in Austria (1710-1725) and then in Germany,
returning to Lombardy after 1737. Moving from baroque to rococo, Carlone proved
himself to be a remarkable master at coordinating colors and of spatial effects, as this
painted draft reveals. Faithful to the precepts of the Council of Trent, Carlone produces an
expressive and accessible composition in which the Virgin is triumphantly welcomed into
heaven by the Holy Trinity, surrounded by a symphony of angels and putti (cherubs).

77

Wolfgang Amadeus Mozart
(1756-1791)

Salzburg, the town of Mozart's birth, was ruled until 1806 by a series of prince-archbishops whose court supported the city's cultural life. Wolfgang Mozart's father, Leopold, served the court for many years as deputy chapel master, and in 1769, the younger Mozart was appointed court concertmaster. The majority of Mozart's sacred works, including his two Vespers settings, date from his years (1769-77 and 1779-81) in the employ of the archbishop.

Hieronymus von Colloredo, who was installed as archbishop in 1772, instituted many reforms, ostensibly in the name of modernization, which had a detrimental effect upon musical life in the city. Colloredo decreed that Mass settings should be shortened and he placed severe restrictions on the use of instrumental music within the liturgy. Mozart and his father both bristled at these new regulations and eagerly sought professional opportunities elsewhere.

Mozart wrote the *Vesperae solennes de confessore* in 1780. As in the *Vesperae solennes de Dominica* (1779), Mozart's setting comprises five psalms and a concluding *Magnificat*. While some of Mozart's Masses from this time reveal a growing complexity in his sacred music, both of the Vespers settings adhere to the guidelines for simplicity and brevity outlined by Colloredo. In accordance with Salzburg tradition, the *Magnificat* heard here opens with a slow introduction. Also in keeping with local custom, Mozart uses the traditional Salzburg instrumentation of strings, bassoon, trumpets, trombones, timpani, and organ. Mozart's setting displays a broad sense of grandeur and exultation rather than a more detailed approach to the text.

And Mary said:

"HE HAS SHOWN THE STRENGTH OF HIS ARM, HE HAS SCATTERED THE PROUD IN THEIR CONCEIT."

The Scriptures often demonstrate that God's ways are not our ways, or our thoughts his thoughts (see Isaiah 55: 8). Who could have guessed that the Christ Child would be born in a stable, perhaps the only place where a poor shepherd could approach a newborn king? Who would have imagined that he would grow up in Nazareth? Why did he choose four fishermen, a tax collector, and a doubter to be among his chosen Twelve? It is clear that God loves the little ones. He sought out the poor, the blind, the deaf, the lost, the lepers, and the lame. He ate with those dismissed as sinners. Jesus, taught well by his mother, rejoices that the Father has hidden from the learned and the clever what he has revealed to merest children (see Luke 10: 21).

The conceited of the world assume that they understand things. They disdain notions of docility and obedience as beneath their dignity. The proud feel no need to ponder, for they acknowledge no mysteries. They hide their insecurities behind a smokescreen of professionalism, competence, and shrewd analysis. They become conceited because they have lost the outward glance required by love. They fail to realize that to grasp anything about God, one must first be grasped by Him. St. Thomas Aquinas confirms this in his teaching on the Holy Spirit's gift of wisdom. Wisdom, Aquinas notes, perfects neither faith nor knowledge; wisdom perfects charity. The intellect does not find its perfection in discursive reasoning, but in the contemplation of God.

Previous page:
Benedictine Abbey Church in Ettal, Bavaria, Germany
Enrico Zuccalli (1642-1724)

The white façade of the Benedictine abbey church in Ettal, with its undulating form within a semicircle, hardly looks like a traditional façade. The dome, set back slightly, nearly gives the impression of real movement, like that of theater stage machinery. Visitors have access to the inside through the central door alone, for the side-doors serve a merely decorative function. The columns frame niches housing the twelve apostles. The cupola is set upon a drum with reinforced buttresses and it mirrors the church's interior layout. Against all expectation from the exterior, that layout is round—yet another baroque illusion devised by the Swiss architect Enrico Zuccalli. The church shelters a lovely white marble statue of the Virgin, affectionately dubbed the "Mother of Kindness."

Contemplation orders the affections and directs the will toward the mystery too beautiful to be true. How fitting that we invoke the Mother of God as the Seat of Wisdom, for "Mary kept all these things, reflecting on them in her heart" (Luke 2: 19).

What is the strength that has "scattered the proud in their conceit"? It is love. When confronted with the Cross, that ultimate gift and victory of Love, argument and logic fail. Only love is strong enough to perceive the triumph of the Cross.

For stern as death is love,
relentless as the nether world
is devotion;
its flames are a blazing fire.
Deep waters cannot quench love,
nor floods sweep it away.

Were one to offer all he owns
to purchase love,
he would be roundly mocked.
Song of Songs 8: 6-7

As St. Paul puts it: "Where is the wise man? Where is the scribe? Where is the debater of the age? Has not God made foolish the wisdom of the world?… We preach Christ crucified" (1 Corinthians 1: 20, 23). St. Augustine too would exclaim, "Give me someone who loves, he will understand me!" God has "shown the strength of his arm" by stretching it out upon the Cross. Under that same arm of the Cross, he gives us our Mother. We join St. Thérèse of the Child Jesus in proclaiming: "O how I love the Blessed Virgin; she is more of a mother than a queen."

At left:
The Assumption (1717)
Egid Quirin Asam (1692-1750)
Detail of the high altar of the Rohr monastery, Bavaria, Germany
White and gilded stucco

Borne aloft by two angels in her Assumption to heaven, this Virgin seems to float in space. Try as one may, the viewer never sees how she manages to stay suspended in air. This miracle of baroque illusion is made possible by the lightness of stucco, a mix of plaster and powdered marble bound with animal or vegetal glue, in vogue among sculptors of this era in Bavaria and Austria. The Virgin of the Assumption was made in 1717 by a master of the genre, Egid Quirin Asam. He and his brother, Cosmas Damian, decorated Southern German churches according to the rules of theatrum sacrum, the artful arrangement of the truths of the faith, following the recommendations of the Council of Trent. The Virgin of Rohr seems to be singing as she rises to heaven. Such an effect is also typical of baroque art, which is inseparable from music, be it secular opera or sacred oratorio.

Next page:
St. Mary's Church (1732 -1739), Dießen am Ammersee, Bavaria, Germany

The baroque Church of St. Mary in Dießen, which looks out over the Ammersee lake, is well known for the magnificence of its stuccoes, gildings, and putti, those chubby cherubs that flit about on high. The church's layout is specific to the baroque: no side altars, no transept, no ambulatory, no way of getting behind the high altar. This unique nave conforms to the rules of the Counter-Reformation: the attention of the faithful must be able to focus on the altar as the place of sacrifice, and on the pulpit (set up in the nave) as the place of preaching.

And Mary said:

"HE HAS CAST DOWN THE MIGHTY
FROM THEIR THRONES,
AND HAS LIFTED UP
THE LOWLY."

Charles Gounod
(1818-1893)

In 1839, Charles Gounod won the coveted Prix de Rome, the highest honor in composition offered by the Paris Conservatoire. As with many other aspiring French composers, the award launched Gounod's career, providing him with three years of study in Rome. In Italy, Gounod fell in love with the music that he heard in the Sistine Chapel—an encounter that sparked his lifelong interest in the composition of sacred music. Returning home in 1843, Gounod found work as chapel master at a Parisian seminary and continued to focus on the composition and performance of music for the liturgy. Briefly, Gounod entertained the notion of becoming a priest, but he abandoned this pursuit in 1848 to devote himself to composition.

For the next two decades, Gounod turned his attention to opera and composed his two great successes, *Faust* (1859) and *Roméo et Juliette* (1867). Fleeing from the turmoil of the Franco-Prussian war, Gounod moved to England in 1870, where he remained for several years. His early interest in sacred music served him well in England, a nation in which choral singing was central to the musical culture. Responding to native musical tastes, Gounod produced a *Magnificat* and *Nunc Dimittis* (published together as *An Evening Service*) for use in the Anglican service of Evensong. Gounod's *Magnificat* is functional liturgical music in its purest form. In writing the piece, Gounod was responding to a practical need. For busy choirmasters looking for an elegant and straightforward setting requiring minimal rehearsal, Gounod's *Magnificat* was surely an attractive addition to the repertoire of English church music.

Previous page (88-89):
The Angelus *(1857-1859)*
Jean-François Millet (1814-1875)
Oil on canvas, 55.5 × 66 cm (21.8 × 26 in.)

A man and a woman pray the Angelus in the evening calm. They have stopped digging up potatoes to do so. Alone in the foreground, in the middle of an immense and empty plain, the peasant couple acquire monumental proportions despite the modest dimensions of the canvas. Their faces remain in the shade, while the light underscores their recollected gestures and demeanor. In the distance one barely makes out the village bell tower. The scene is neither anecdotal nor aesthetic; for Millet, himself the son of peasants and ever a man of simple tastes, this scene is intimately bound up with the meaning of life, a continuity in keeping with the great rhythms of creation. His painting attains a universal significance because it does not set the two figures in a falsely pastoral décor; rather they are two peasants in a natural setting, accepting their mortal condition in humility and gratitude within the daily patterns of work, family life, and religious observance. Transcending mere sentimentality, Millet imbues this painting with a sacred and quasi-mystical character.

Previous page (91):
The Sacré-Cœur Basilica in Montmartre, view from rue Lafitte *(1890)*
After Paul Heydel (1854-?)
Engraved and colored wood

This surprising view of the Montmartre basilica can be seen even today, from the end of rue Lafitte and the intersection with boulevard Haussmann. From such a vantage point the Sacré-Cœur of Montmartre looks as though it has been set on top of Our Lady of Loretto Church, when in fact it lies a good distance away from it. Our Lady of Loretto, masterpiece of the neoclassical architect Hippolyte Lebas, was built between 1823 and 1836; it is modeled on the basilicas of Rome. A symbol of Paris the world over, the Sacré-Cœur basilica, located at the summit of the Montmartre hill, was erected after the French National Assembly voted in July 1873, to thank the Sacred Heart of Jesus for its protection during the 1870-71 Franco-Prussian war. The basilica and its central dome, over which looms the bell tower housing "la Savoyarde," a nineteen-ton bell, are sparkling white. Since 1885 perpetual adoration of the Blessed Sacrament has gone on uninterrupted.

The poet Virgil, a lowly farmer's son, is regarded as the greatest poet of ancient Rome. In his *Eclogue 4*, written some forty years before Christ, he refers to the birth of a man sent down from heaven, who would make justice return, do away with our old wickedness, and "free the earth from never-ceasing fear."* Modern scholars argue that he wrote in praise of Augustus Caesar, whose reign initiated the *Pax Romana*. Others, including St. Augustine and Dante, see Virgil as a "natural Christian," a pagan prophesying the birth of Christ.

Regardless of who is correct, the fact remains that the mighty have long abused their power.

That justice should descend from a mortal throne seems an exceptional situation indeed. King Herod the Great, only months after Mary first prayed the *Magnificat*, would order the slaughter of the Innocents of Bethlehem. Herod Antipas, his son, beheaded John the Baptist, and, during the Passion, sent Jesus back to Pilate for execution. Since both Herods colluded with the Romans, it is easy to understand why faithful Jews, who always felt "lowly" compared to other nations, assumed that the Messiah would free them from political tyranny.

The Poems of Virgil, trans. James Rhoades (Chicago: *Encyclopedia Britannica*, 1952), 14.

Burial at Ornans *(1849)*
Gustave Courbet (1819-1877)
Oil on canvas, 311 × 668 cm (122.5 × 263 in.)

*Courbet's canvas, extraordinary in its size—
nearly seven yards long—presents a very
realistic gallery of forty-six figures. He drew
his inspiration from seventeenth-century
Dutch group portraits. On the other hand,
he used dimensions usually reserved for
the "noble" genre of historical painting. By
depicting an everyday subject in this form
Courbet shocked his contemporaries, who
denounced the trivial character of his figures.
Future generations would judge it to be a
milestone in the history of art. Either way it
is impossible to remain indifferent before this
work in which blacks and whites dominate,
barely punctuated by a few rich reds
embellishing the parish officers and altar boys.
The painter represents this scene at the specific
moment when the procession of mourners
has just entered the cemetery of Ornans,
Courbet's native village, and has divided into
three groups: the priest's attendants, men, and
women. One's gaze is drawn to the middle
of the canvas, near the gravedigger kneeling
near the fresh grave he has just dug. Although
his face is turned toward the priest and the
cross, drawing us into the ceremony's spiritual
universe, the rest of his body is angled
toward the grave, reminding us of the passing
world here below and the reality of death.*

At left:
The Church of Auvers-sur-Oise, *(1890)*
Vincent van Gogh (1853-1890)
Oil on canvas, 94 × 74,5 cm (37 × 29 in.)

*After leaving the South of France, Arles,
and the hospital in Saint-Rémy de Provence,
Vincent Van Gogh settled in Auvers-sur-Oise.
He lived near the house of Doctor Gachet,
an amateur painter and friend to the
Impressionists. In the two months that elapsed
between his arrival on May 21, 1890 and his
death on July 29, Vincent produced close to
seventy paintings, amounting to more than
one per day. The church of Auvers-sur-Oise
was built in the thirteenth century along
Gothic lines; yet under the artist's brush it
becomes a flamboyant monument animated
with its own life. The back-lit church stands
out against a cobalt blue sky that is itself
in palpable motion, a characteristic of
the painter's style in his waning years.
His brushstrokes seem etched in matter.
A woman's figure passes by without paying
attention to the church; she is walking
fast on a path that seems to be moving
forward as well. The clock on the bell
tower has no hands. In an exploration
of time and duration, immanence and
change, Van Gogh has painted metaphysical
contrasts that reflect his own destiny.*

In their own history, the son of a Hebrew slave led them out of Egypt to the promised land. A shepherd boy, the littlest son of Jesse, slew Goliath and reigned as king for nearly forty years. A woman delivered the Israelites from a mighty captain of the Canaanite army.

> *Blessed among women be Jael,*
> *blessed among tent-dwelling*
> *women...*
> *With her left hand*
> *she reached for the peg,*
> *with her right,*
> *for the workman's mallet.*
> *She hammered Sisera,*
> *crushed his head;*
> *she smashed, stove in his temple.*
> *Judges 5: 24-26*

When the God-Man broke into history, however, he turned the logic of violence upside down. Yes, he would establish his kingdom through the shedding of blood, but the blood would be his own. Allowing his own body to be pierced by nail and mallet, he became a "stumbling block to Jews and foolishness to Gentiles" (1 Corinthians 1: 23). Simeon's prophecy only confirmed what Mary already expressed in the *Magnificat*. The Lord's lowly handmaid understood the contradiction her son would represent, and she foresaw the piercing of her heart (see Luke 2: 34-35).

Our hearts are the thrones the Lord most desires, and the thrones we most fiercely defend. Christ the King comes to liberate us from our self-reliance, our agendas, our sins. The dying required is death to self. We must come to echo St. Paul's assertion: "It is no longer I who live, but Christ who lives in me" (Galatians 2: 20). Mary's prayers embolden us in the battle against principalities and powers, in our own battle for prayer (see Ephesians 6: 12). Mary knows that her son is the high priest able, as the Letter to the Hebrews puts it, "to sympathize with our weakness" (Hebrews 4: 15). As Moses encouraged the Israelites, she whispers to us, "The Lord himself will fight for you; you have only to keep still" (Exodus 14: 14).

At right:
The Visitation (1857)
Stained glass
Notre Dame Church, Casteljaloux, France

The stained glass windows of the collegiate church of Casteljaloux, which was built in the twelfth and thirteenth centuries, are dedicated to the Virgin. They were made in the Gothic style but date to as late as 1857. Destroyed by the Protestants in September 1568, the church was rebuilt in the seventeenth century. Its façade and bell tower were not completed until the eighteenth century. The lively colors and idealized faces are characteristic of neo-Gothic style. Nineteenth-century artists drew their inspiration from the Middle Ages in reviving ornamental floral motifs and stylized branch-patterns, all the while being inspired by the neoclassical style. In keeping with the taste and religious fervor of the time, the faces and demeanors of Elizabeth and the Virgin express both the purity of the feminine ideal and the splendor of Christian charity.

FOURNI
PAR DIVERS

Charles Villiers Stanford
(1852-1924)

Born in Dublin, Charles Villiers Stanford was a leading figure of the so-called English musical renaissance of the late nineteenth century. Trained in Cambridge and Berlin, Stanford held concurrent appointments at Cambridge and the Royal College of Music while maintaining an active career as a composer. With his wide-reaching influence, Stanford made an invaluable contribution to the rehabilitation of English music in the waning years of the Victorian era. Throughout much of the nineteenth century, England was derided by continental observers as the "land without music." Musical tastes were inclined toward parlor songs and other popular genres, standards for the performance of church music were embarrassingly low, and serious composition had at best a marginal place in English musical culture. Stanford changed all of this—reinventing the idea of the "English" composer and paving the way for the achievements of Holst, Vaughan Williams, Howells, Britten, and so many other distinguished English composers of the twentieth century. Indeed, his role as a teacher of two generations of English musicians is perhaps the most important part of his legacy.

As a composer, Stanford was active in many genres, but he is remembered primarily for his Anglican choral music. The *Evening Service in G Major*, written in 1902, is one of Stanford's best-loved settings of the *Magnificat* and the *Nunc Dimittis*. In his *Magnificat*, Mary's "voice" is represented by a solo soprano. The beautiful unfolding of the Virgin's song is punctuated by entrances of the full chorus and supported throughout by a bubbling organ accompaniment that captures the joyful obedience and gentle exuberance of the text.

And Mary said:

"HE HAS FILLED THE HUNGRY WITH GOOD
THINGS, AND THE RICH
HE HAS SENT AWAY EMPTY."

Previous page:
The Virgin with Host *(1854)*
Jean-Auguste-Dominique Ingres (1780-1867)
Oil on canvas (tondo), diameter: 113 cm (44.5 in.)

The Virgin with Host is a circular painting in the style of Renaissance tondi (round paintings). She is recollected before the host of her Son's flesh. "The Holy Virgin, holding her beautiful hands joined together by the tips of her long fingers, with her eyes adores... the host, a white sun shining atop the chalice where, in unplumbed mystery, the son she just now held in her arms is incarnate; the Madonna's head is divine in its sweetness. Her pure features, of a Christianized Greek type, bear an incomparable nobility that is the special preserve of Mr. Ingres," wrote the poet and novelist Théophile Gautier. This nineteenth-century comment exemplifies the devotion of its time, which is expressed in holy images celebrating both the Mother of God and the beauty of woman. Beyond this, however, the fervor of a great Marian century shines through, a piety nourished by many apparitions: in 1830 to Catherine Labouré in the rue du Bac in Paris; in 1846 to the two young shepherds at La Salette. The year that Ingres completed his painting, Pope Pius IX pronounced the dogma of the Immaculate Conception. Mary was soon to appear at Lourdes (1858).

I n the realm of the flesh, hunger signals the need for sustenance. In the spiritual realm, hunger is the desire for God, the very sustenance of our existence. St. Augustine called this hunger the "restlessness" of our hearts, the desire to know Him in whose image we are created. These words, "He has filled the hungry with good things," assure us that the deepest longings of our hearts, our spiritual longings, which only God can satisfy, do not end in frustration. Jesus himself proclaimed, in his Sermon on the Mount, "Blessed are those who hunger and thirst for righteousness, for they will be satisfied" (Matthew 5: 6).

Certain traditions in Catholic spirituality seem to argue that the hunger of desire is, at best, dangerous. Our disordered desires may lead us to lesser goods, or even into sin. It would seem that the holy Virgin of Virgins should prefer to be left empty, hungry, and unfulfilled. However, his type of asceticism more closely approaches a Stoic or Buddhist sentiment than a Christian one. The enemy is not hunger but the disordered appetites. The true danger lies not in desire itself but in our capacity to desire creatures more than the Creator.

The desires for God, however, are the wings of the soul. St. Augustine, the man who once felt it was inappropriate for him to weep at his mother's funeral, says, "The whole of the Christian life is a holy desire." St. Katherine Drexel once remarked, "I looked up in wonder at God's wonderful ways and thought how little we imagine what may be the result of listening and acting on a desire God puts into the heart... Yes, nourish before him great desires."

Left page:
The Visitation
Frédéric Montenard (1849-1926)
Fresco
Saint-François-de-Sales Church, Paris, France

The realism and simplicity of this Visitation scene invite the viewer to live out, if only in spirit, this sacred moment in its actual conditions. The landscape, buildings, and costumes evoke the Mediterranean world. Frédéric Montenard, who was born into an old Provençal family, was in the habit of placing Southern French panoramas in his large decorative compositions. Besides his landscapes and seascapes, he is also known for his panels in the Sainte-Baume chapel in the Var (Southern France) that depicts the life of St. Mary Magdalene.

St. John of the Cross, who seems to recommend desiring *nada*, has this to say about prayer:

Great talent is a gift from God, but it is a gift which is by no means necessary in order to pray well. This gift is required in order to converse well with men; but it is not necessary in order to speak well with God. For that, one needs good desires, and nothing more.

The Lord himself said from the Cross, "I thirst" (John 19: 28). His thirst for our righteousness is our salvation.

Among the antiphons for the Canticle of Mary found in the Liturgy of the Hours, one reads: "If you hunger for holiness, God will satisfy your longing, good measure and flowing over." God invites all to the blessed banquet of faith.

Above:
Holy Name Cathedral (1874-1875), *Chicago, Illinois, USA*

The cathedral of Chicago has grown more beautiful with time. Since the foundation stone was set in 1874, successive renovations have altered its original appearance and have graced the nave with a lithe and luminous quality. Originally built in a neo-Gothic style on architect Patrick Charles Keely's blueprint, Holy Name Cathedral was still under construction at the time of its consecration in 1875. Thirteen years later a restoration campaign was already deemed necessary. At this time the wooden pillars were replaced by pink St. Baum marble columns, and the plaster ceiling vaults were torn down to reveal the original walnut and oak ribs and panels that we see lavishly decorated here. Structural reinforcement in cement and steel closed the cathedral in 1968. In 1989 a new organ from the workshops of Dutch organ maker Flentrop Orgelbouw was installed above the gallery. Its double case was carved in oak and partially gilded in the Dutch tradition. Closed for six months after a blaze caused serious damage to the roof, the newly renovated cathedral reopened its doors for worship on August 1, 2009.

103

God desires that we come with hunger and longing, ready to be filled. Mary shared her son's conviction: "My food is to do the will of the one who sent me" (John 4: 34). With her *fiat*, she has prepared the meal that really satisfies. Mary, herself *full* of grace, hungers for our sanctification. St. Joseph of Cupertino said of her:

My mother is very strange; if I bring her flowers, she says she does not want them; if I bring her cherries, she will not take them, and if I then ask her what she desires, she replies: "I desire your heart, for I live on hearts."

At right:
Magnificat *(1909)*
Maurice Denis (1870-1943)
Oil on canvas, 130 × 140 cm (51 × 55 in.)

Maurice Denis chose to depict the two cousins' silent encounter, just moments before Elizabeth's greeting and Mary's Magnificat. It is an ineffable moment of revelation when the Spirit of God shed his light upon the universe. The scene takes place on the balcony of the Silencio villa, which Maurice Denis purchased in Brittany from Perros-Guirrec in late August 1908. The magnificent sunsets on the ocean and the bay of Trestrignel inspired his Magnificat. He included a chapel in the landscape as a reminder that Mary, having become the "Temple of the Holy Spirit" of the litanies of the Virgin, symbolizes the new Church. A young girl holds a candle whose flame expresses the lasting value of the sacred message for present-day witnesses. The painter produced several Visitation scenes, linking each to a pregnancy in his family: towards the end of 1908, his wife Marthe was expecting their sixth child, who was born on August 11, 1909, at Silencio.

At left:
St. Patrick's Cathedral *(1858-1879)*
viewed from Rockefeller Center
New York, NY, USA

*In the heart of Manhattan,
a stone's throw from
Rockefeller Center, St. Patrick's
Cathedral dominates Fifth
Avenue. With its cross-shaped
layout and three naves, it is the
largest neo-Gothic cathedral of
the Americas. It was built out
of white marble quarried in
New York and Massachusetts
following James Renwick Jr.'s
architectural blueprint. The
foundation stone was laid on
August 15, 1858 in an area that still
had a relatively low population.
Archbishop John Joseph Hughes,
persuaded that the location would
someday lie at the heart of the
city, stuck to his project despite
setback after setback, including
the Civil War. Thanks to the
generosity of 103 citizens who gave
$1,000 each, and thanks to the
equal generosity of thousands of
poor Irish immigrants who gave
a penny apiece, the archbishop's
vision finally came to fruition.
The cathedral, completed in
1878, was consecrated on May
25, 1879. Its 330 foot-tall bell
towers were completed in 1888.*

Arvo Pärt
(born 1935)

Arvo Pärt is something of an anomaly among contemporary "classical" composers. Recordings of his music have sold millions of copies, and even conservative listeners who scoff at "modern" music find something in Pärt's style that speaks to them. To say that Pärt's music is popular is not to suggest that it panders to low tastes. Indeed, it is remarkable that Pärt has managed to devise a style of such wide and immediate appeal while also maintaining an uncompromising allegiance to his own artistic standards.

Born in Estonia in 1935 and trained at the conservatory in Talinn, Pärt grew up under the long shadow of the Soviet state. In the 1960s, his exploration of contemporary, Western techniques of composition, together with his growing interest in religious music, earned him official rebuke from the government. After reassessing his work in the 1970s, Pärt studied Gregorian chant, emerging from this period with a desire to write music of daring simplicity. In adopting a new economy of means, Pärt aligned himself with the minimalist trend then emerging in much American music while forging an approach that was uniquely his own.

Pärt combines the simplicity and rhythmic fluidity of chant with an expanded harmonic vocabulary to create music that seems at once remote and immediate. Pärt's embrace of static textures allows the listener a new freedom to engage deeply in the moment of the music. He has said that "it is enough when a single note is beautifully played," and, in works like the *Magnificat*, he demonstrates his faith in this ideal. Pärt's music, much of it the product of his own deeply held religious beliefs, evokes a quality of contemplative spirituality welcomed by many listeners.

And Mary said:

"HE HAS COME TO THE HELP
OF HIS SERVANT ISRAEL
FOR HE HAS REMEMBERED HIS PROMISE OF
MERCY, THE PROMISE HE MADE TO
OUR FATHERS, TO ABRAHAM
AND HIS CHILDREN FOR EVER."

What was the promise made to Abraham? God promised him a family. He promised that Abraham would be the father of a great nation, and that through his progeny all the nations of the world would be blessed. This promise was made long before the birth of Isaac. Later, as if he were taking back this promise, God asked Abraham to sacrifice his son. If, as Mary tells us, God has remembered his promise of mercy, does that also mean that he can forget it?

We live in a world strewn with broken promises. Relationships, like so many old appliances, seem to be disposable today. We make commitments with great trepidation, and only after years of careful consideration. Our noisy lives too often distract us from following through on good intentions. The world moves so quickly that everything seems to change; nothing seems stable and sure.

God, though, does not forget his promises. The Scriptures call him our "rock."

God alone is my rock and my salvation, my secure height;
I shall not fall.
My safety and glory are with God,
my strong rock and refuge.

Psalm 62: 7-8

In fact, God continues to renew his promise. His light "shines in the darkness, and the darkness has not overcome it" (John 1: 5). God's promise to Abraham is fulfilled in Christ, and in the family of God we call the Church. The real promise is eternal life. Every time we recite the Creed, we profess our faith in God's promise of mercy.

In a covenant, as in a marriage, there are two parties. The Old Testament recounts the roller-coaster history of God's marriage to Israel. Time and time again Israel broke the covenant, but God did not abandon his people. Instead, he bound himself even more closely to the human family, by a bond that can never be broken (see Eucharistic Prayer for Reconciliation I). That bond began in the wonderful exchange that took place in the womb of the Virgin.

God's restless heart, so to speak, found a resting place in her. She is the faithful and spotless bride who always says "yes" to her Lord.

At right:
Achtyrka, the Red Church (before 1908 or 1917)
Vassily Kandinsky (1866-1944)
Oil on wood, 28 × 19.2 cm (11 × 7.5 in.)

Kandinsky was fond of painting in the Achtyrka region near Moscow, where his sister-in-law owned a property, and he returned there on several occasions in his career. He certainly stayed there in 1901, when he began open-air painting. He began travelling to Europe in 1906, after which his painting increasingly tended toward abstraction and his colors grew much brighter. He produced his first abstract painting in 1910. Yet from 1914 and 1924 Kandinsky returned to Russia, where he engaged in figurative painting again for a short period. Does this view of the Red Church date from this period, between 1914 and 1917, or rather from some time before 1908? Scholarly opinions vary; however, this uncertainty in no way diminishes the poetry that radiates from this sketch. Kandinsky here plays on contrasts: the upright trees and church are juxtaposed to the horizontal lines of the lawn and riverbank; the flat tint of the grass is an invitation to rest, while in the foreground the vibrant reflections in the water create a subtle impression of movement.

The Christian commitment is rooted in God's promise of mercy and in our baptismal promises. In the Rite of Christian Initiation, the Elect ask the Church for faith, confident that the sacraments offer them God's promise of eternal life. Keeping our vows is never easy. With Mary's aid, we strive to renew and keep our promises. In her, we find hope on our pilgrimage. St. Bernard of Clairvaux teaches us that those who invoke Mary will never be disappointed.

In dangers, in troubles, in doubts, think of Mary, call upon Mary... If you follow her guidance, you will not go astray. If you pray to her, you will not give up hope. If you think of her, you will not go wrong. With your hand in hers, you will never stumble. With her protecting you, you will not be afraid. With her leading you, you will reach the goal. Her kindness will see you through to the end.

At left:
Cathedral of Our Lady of the Angels, *(1999-2002)*
Los Angeles, California, USA
José Rafael Moneo Vallés (born 1937)
Cross-shaped stained-glass window
Alabaster and concrete

The light of God is revealed to the world through the sacrifice of Christ on the Cross. José Rafael Moneo Vallés, the Spanish architect, seeks to express this theological truth in the gigantic concrete cross overhanging the altar of the Cathedral of Our Lady of the Angels in Los Angeles. Natural light, filtered through the windows' alabaster slabs, floods the wide sanctuary; here four hundred priests can gather around the bishop to concelebrate the Liturgy. The alabaster is veined with streaks of red, grey, yellow, and green, and was especially imported from Spain to trim all of the cathedral's stained-glass windows. As a result, they shed a milky and warm light that is conducive to prayer. When lit at night, these alabaster windows can be glimpsed from great distances. Built between 1999 and 2002 to replace the former cathedral of Saint Vibiana, which had suffered damage in the 1994 earthquake, the Cathedral of Our Lady of the Angels can accommodate up to three thousand people.

At left:
Mary and Elizabeth
Dorothy Webster Hawksley (1884-1970)
Tempera on wooden panel, 50.8 × 34.3 cm (20 × 13.5 in.)

*The soft, subtle colors of this encounter between Mary and Elizabeth
convey a particularly soothing atmosphere in this scene. The young
Virgin is simultaneously composed yet still stunned by the wonders
the Almighty has done for her. Meanwhile, Elizabeth speaks to
her with profound sympathy. At the center of the composition
the light accentuates the gently intertwining hands of two cousins.
Dorothy Webster Hawksley, a talented yet little-known artist,
lived in London all her life. Drawing on the influence of Japanese
prints and Italian painters of the early Renaissance, she developed a
resolutely personal style, marked by tranquility and clarity, a delicate
sensitivity, and figures imbued with contemplative solitude.*

Above:
Notre-Dame-du-Haut Chapel, Ronchamp, France (1955)
Le Corbusier (1885-1965)

"In building this chapel I wanted to create a place of silence, of peace, of inner joy," wrote
architect Le Corbusier about Ronchamp. This definition corresponds well to the impression
one receives inside the building. Breaking from the traditional cruciform plan, Le Corbusier
opted for an asymmetrical layout: a single hall, without aisle or transept. The light,
which is either white or colored according to the time of day, filters through openings in
the thick concrete wall to the south. Le Corbusier himself painted the glass windows in
primary colors. Notre-Dame-du-Haut is perched above the Belfort Pass, where it replaces
the neo-Gothic pilgrimage church that was bombed out in 1944. He was commissioned to
build it between 1950 and 1955 at the behest of the Religious Art Commission. Under the
leadership of Fathers Couturier and Régamey, this commission promoted a far-reaching
program of religious building in a contemporary spirit in the years following the war.

TABLE OF CONTENTS

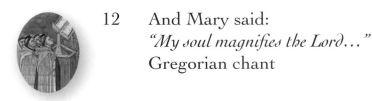

70   And Mary said:
"He has mercy on those who fear him in every generation."
Georg Philipp Telemann (1681-1767)

78   And Mary said:
"He has shown the strength of his arm, he has scattered the proud in their conceit."
Wolfgang Amadeus Mozart (1756-1791)

88   And Mary said:
"He has cast down the mighty from their thrones, and has lifted up the lowly."
Charles Gounod (1818-1893)

98   And Mary said:
"He has filled the hungry with good things, and the rich he has sent away empty."
Charles Villiers Stanford (1852-1924)

108   And Mary said:
"He has come to the help of his servant Israel for he has remembered his promise of mercy, the promise he made to our fathers, to Abraham and his children for ever."
Arvo Pärt (born 1935)

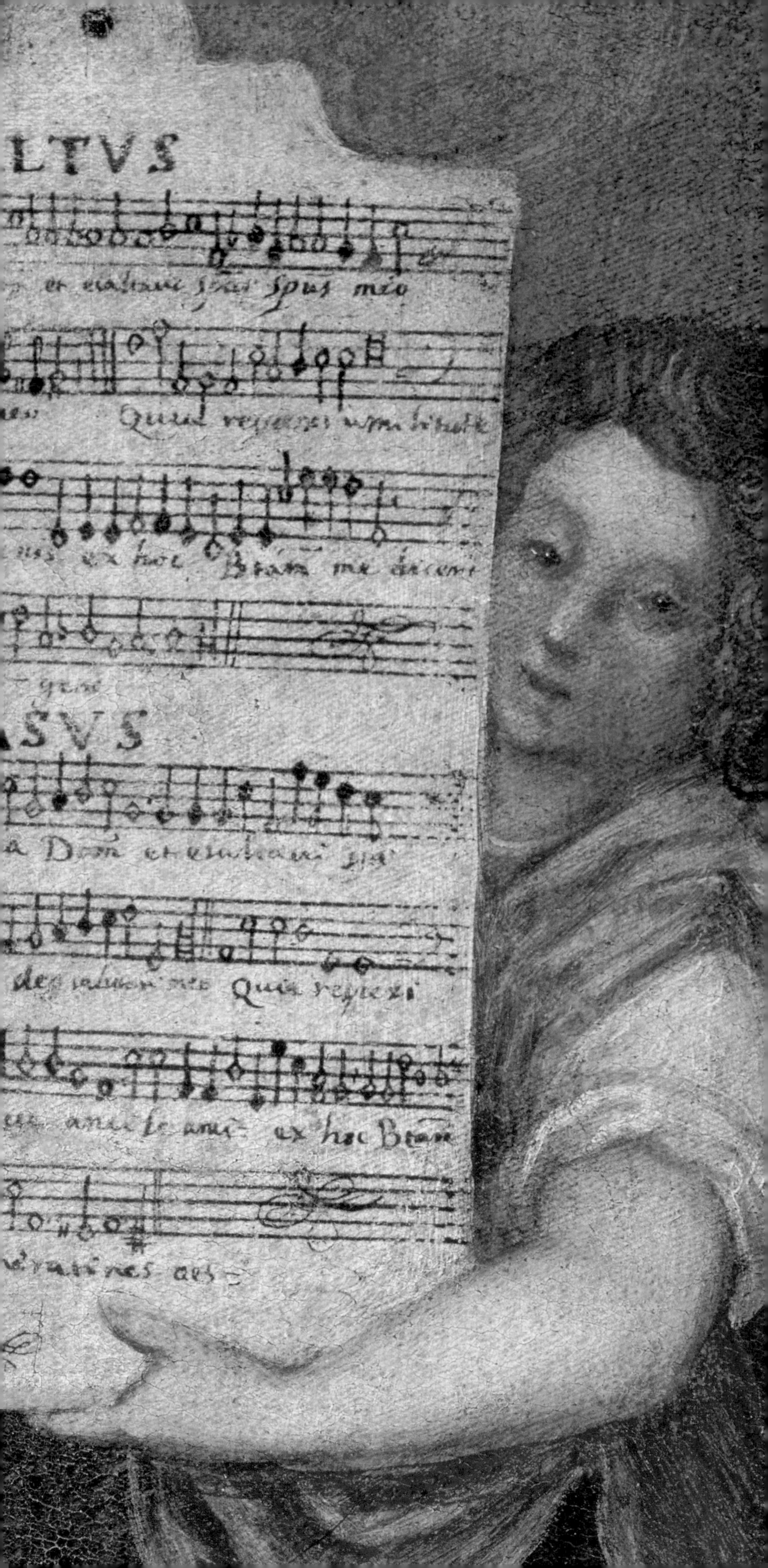

LTVS
SVS

AUDIO CREDITS

1 – *Magnificat* (Tone IV) with Antiphon: *Rubum quem viderat*
Benedictine Monks of Santo Domingo de Silos, Spain
Excerpt from Jade CD "Christmas Chants in Silos"
© and ℗ 1996 Editions Jade

2 – *Magnificat sexti toni*
Adrian Willaert (1490-1562)
Oxford Camerata
Conductor: Jeremy Summerly
℗ Naxos – HNH International

3 – *Magnificat a 12*
Giovanni Gabrieli (1557-1612)
Studio de Musique ancienne de Montréal, Concertino Palatino
Direction: Christopher Jackson
Disque ATMA classique

4 – *Magnificat* from the Short Service
Orlando Gibbons (1583-1625)
Oxford Camerata
Conductor: Jeremy Summerly
℗ Naxos – HNH International

5 – *Magnificat*
Tomás de Torrejón y Velasco (1644-1728)
Coro de Niños Cantores de Córdoba
Ensemble Elyma
Direction: Gabriel Garrido
Excerpt from « Musiques des Missions et Cathédrales Andines »
K.617123
© K617

6 – *Magnificat* (H. 76)
Marc-Antoine Charpentier (1643-1704)
Les Pages et les Chantres, Centre de Musique Baroque de Versailles
Conductor: Olivier Schneebeli
℗ Alpha

7 – *Deutsche Magnificat*
Georg Philipp Telemann (1681-1767)
CV 83.180 ℗ Coproduction
Südwestrundfunk – Carus
© Carus-Verlag Stuttgart

SWR⟩⟩　　**Ⲵ Carus**

8 – *Magnificat* from the *Vesperae solennes de confessore* (K. 339)
Wolfgang Amadeus Mozart (1756-1791)
Capella Brugensis & Collegium Instrumentale Brugense
Conductor: Patrick Peire
℗ Naxos – HNH International

9 – *Magnificat* from *An Evening Service*
Charles Gounod (1818-1893)
CV 83.161
© Carus-Verlag Stuttgart

Ⲵ Carus

10 – *Magnificat* from the *Evening Service in G major*, Op. 81
Charles Villiers Stanford (1852-1924)
St. John's College Choir, Cambridge
Conductor: Christopher Robinson
℗ Naxos – HNH International

11 – *Magnificat*
Arvo Pärt (born 1935)
Elora Festival Singers
Conductor: Noel Edison
℗ Naxos – HNH International

ART CREDITS

Cover and pages 10-11: *Virgin with Child and Five Angels* (called *the Madonna of the Magnificat*), Sandro Botticelli (1445-1510), Uffizi Gallery, Florence, Italy. © akg-images / Erich Lessing.

Page 12: Illumination, German Miniature, Initial with Seven Singing Carmelites - Missal 570, fol. 34 r, 15th c., San Marco Museum, Forence, Italy. © akg-images / Rabatti - Domingie.

Page 13: *The Visitation*, Master of Lluçà, 13th c., Episcopal Museum, Vic, Catalonia, Spain. © The Art Archive / Episcopal Museum Vic Catalonia / Gianni Dagli Orti.

Page 15: Smiling Angel (detail), 13th c., Notre Dame Cathedral, Rheims, France. © akg-images / Jean-Paul Dumontier.

Pages 16-17: *The Visitation*, 12th c., Notre Dame Cathedral, Chartres, France. © La Collection / Jean-Paul Dumontier.

Page 18: Notre Dame Cathedral, Rheims, France, 13th c. © La Collection / Jean-Paul Dumontier.

Page 20: Abbey Church of Sainte-Foy, Conques, France, 11-12th c. © akg-images / Bildarchiv Monheim.

Pages 22-23: Cloister of the Monastery of Santo Domingo de Silos, Spain, 11-12th c. © The Art Archive / Monastery of Santo Domingo de Silos, Spain / Gianni Dagli Arti.

Page 24: *Portrait of Adrian Willaert*, International Museum and Music Library, Bologna, Italy. © Photo Scala, Florence.

Page 25: *The Visitation*, Flemish School, 16th c., Private Collection. © Joanna Booth / Bridgeman Giraudon.

Page 27: *The Visitation*, Flemish Miniature from the Hastings Book of Hours, 15th c., British Library, London, England. © akg-images / British Library.

Pages 28-29: *The Census in Bethlehem*, Pieter Brueghel the Younger (1564-1638), Bonnefantenmuseum, Maastricht, Netherlands. © akg-images.

Pages 30-31: *Interior of the Antwerp Cathedral*, Hendrik van Steenwijk (1580-1649) and Jan Brueghel the Elder, known as 'Velvet' (1568-1625), Museum of Fine Arts, Budapest, Hungary. © akg-images.

Page 32: *Portrait of Giovanni Gabrieli*, Annibale Carracci (1560-1609), Gemäldegalerie Alte Meister, Dresden, Germany. © Staatliche Kunstsammlungen Dresden / Bridgeman Giraudon.

Page 33: *The Pietà*, Michelangelo Buonarroti (1475-1564), St. Peter's Basilica, Rome, Vatican City. © akg-images.

Pages 34-35: View of Rome, Italy. © Cuboimages / Leemage.

Page 37: Interior view of St. Peter's Basilica, Rome, Vatican City. © akg-images / Erich Lessing.

Pages 38-39: *The Visitation*, Paolo Caliari, called Veronese (1528-1588), Galleria dell'Accademia, Venice, Italy. © Cameraphoto Arte Venezia / Bridgeman Giraudon.

Pages 40-41: View of Venice, Italy. © Hervé Champollion / akg-images.

Page 42: *Portrait of Orlando Gibbons*, English school, 17th c., Faculty of Music Collection, Oxford University, England. © Bridgeman Giraudon.

Page 43: *The Visitation*, Peter Paul Rubens (1577-1640), Notre Dame Cathedral, Antwerp, Belgium. © akg-images / Erich Lessing.

Page 45: The Nave of Westminster Abbey, London, England, 13-14th c. © akg-images / Roman von Götz.

Pages 46-47: *Music Score of Magnificat by Cornelis Verdonck (1563-1625)*, Martin de Vos

(1532-1603), Music School, Stockholm, Sweden. © akg-images / Erich Lessing.

Pages 48-49: Interior of King's College Chapel, Cambridge, England, 15-16th c. © Bridgeman Giraudon.

Page 52: *Portrait of a gentleman said to be García Hurtado de Mendoza, viceroy of Peru*, Sofonisba Anguissola (attr. to) (c. 1532-1625), Lobkowicz Palace, Prague Castle, Czech Republic. © Bridgeman Giraudon.

Page 53: *Our Lady of Guadalupe*, Anonymous, 18th c., National Palace, Mexico City, Mexico. © The Art Archive / National Palace Mexico City / Gianni Dagli Orti.

Pages 54-55: Cathedral of Our Lady of the Immaculate Conception, Campeche, Mexico. © Imagestate / Leemage.

Pages 56-57: Angels overhanging the altarpiece of St. Joseph Chapel, Mexican School, 18th c., Church of San Francisco Javier, Tepotzotlán, Mexico. © Bridgeman Giraudon.

Pages 58-59: *The Visitation*, José Sanchez, 17th c., Louvre Museum, Paris, France. © RMN / Gérard Blot.

Pages 60-61: Sagrario Metropolitano Church, Mexico City, Mexico, 18th c. © akg-images / Gilles Mermet.

Page 62: *Portrait of Marc-Antoine Charpentier*, Private Collection. © Costa / Leemage.

Page 63: *The Magnificat Madonna*, Jean-Baptiste Jouvenet (1644-1717), Prado Museum, Madrid, Spain. © Bridgeman Giraudon.

Page 64: *Louis XIV*, Hyacinthe Rigaud (1659-1743), Louvre Museum, Paris, France. © akg-images / Joseph Martin.

Pages 66-67: View of Château de Versailles, France. © akg-images / Bildarchiv Monheim.

Page 68: *The Assumption of the Virgin*, Philippe de Champaigne (1602-1674), Museum of Fine Arts, Marseille, France. © Bridgeman Giraudon.

Page 70: *Portrait of Georg Philipp Telemann*, Private Collection. © Fototeca / Leemage.

Page 71: *The Visitation*, Francesco Salvator Fontebasso (1709-1759), Louvre Museum, Paris, France. © RMN / Jean-Gilles Berizzi.

Page 73: *The Visitation*, Ubaldo Gandolfi (1728-1781), Private Collection. © Bonhams, London, UK / Bridgeman Giraudon.

Pages 74-75: *The Assumption of Mary*, Carlo Innocenzo Carlone (1686-1775), SMPK, Gemäldegalerie, Berlin, Germany. © akg-images.

Pages 76-77: Two angels, 18th c., Church of Saint-Martin, Orignac, France. © akg-images / Michel Dieuzaide.

Page 78: *Portrait of Wolfgang Amadeus Mozart*, Barbara Krafft (1764-1825), Society of Music Friends in Vienna, Austria. © The Art Archive / Society Of The Friends Of Music Vienna / Alfredo Dagli Orti.

Page 79: *The Immaculate Conception*, Giovanni Battista Tiepolo (1696-1770), Museo Civico, Vicenza, Italy. © Bridgeman Giraudon.

Page 81: *The Magnificat*, Gabriel-François Doyen (attr. to) (1726-1806), Magnin Museum, Dijon, France. © RMN / René-Gabriel Ojéda.

Pages 82-83: Benedictine Abbey Church in Ettal, Bavaria, Germany, Enrico Zuccali (1642-1724). © akg-images / Schütze / Rodemann.

Page 84: *The Assumption*, Egid Quirin Asam (1692-1750), Monastery of Rohr, Bavaria, Germany. © akg-images / Erich Lessing.

Pages 86-87: Interior of St. Mary's Church, Dießen am Ammersee, Bavaria, Germany, 18th c. © akg-images / Erich Lessing.

Pages 88-89: *The Angelus*, Jean-François Millet (1814-1875), Orsay Museum, Paris, France. © akg-images / Erich Lessing.

Page 90: *Portrait of Charles Gounod*, Felix Eugen (1837-1906). © akg-images.

Page 91: *The Sacré-Cœur Basilica in Montmartre, view from rue Lafitte*, Paul Heydel, 19th c. © akg-images.

Pages 92-93: *Burial at Ornans*, Gustave Courbet (1819-1877), Orsay Museum, Paris, France. © akg-images / Erich Lessing.

Pages 94-95: *The Church of Auvers-sur-Oise*, Vincent Van Gogh (1853-1890), Orsay Museum, Paris, France. © Bridgeman Giraudon.

Pages 97: *The Visitation*, 19th c., Notre Dame Church, Casteljaloux, France. © La Collection / Jean-Paul Dumontier.

Page 98: *Portrait of Charles Villiers Stanford (1852-1924)*. © United Archives / Leemage.

Page 99: *The Virgin with Host*, Jean-Auguste-Dominique Ingres (1780-1867), Orsay Museum, Paris, France. © akg-images / Erich Lessing.

Page 100: *The Visitation*, Frédéric Montenard (1845-1927), Saint-François-de-Sales Church, Paris, France. © Collection Dagli Orti / Gianni Dagli Orti.

Pages 102-103: Interior of Holy Name Cathedral, Chicago, Illinois, USA, 19th c. © akg-images / James Morris.

Pages 104-105: *Magnificat*, Maurice Denis (1870-1943), Private Collection. © Bridgeman Giraudon. © Adagp, Paris 2009.

Pages 106-107: St. Patrick's Cathedral, New York, NY, USA, 19th c. © akg-images / Walter Limot.

Page 108: *Portrait of Arvo Pärt*. © akg-images / Niklaus Stauss.

Page 109: *Mother and Child*, Pablo Picasso (1881-1973), Private Collection. © Bridgeman Giraudon. © Succession Picasso 2009.

Page 110: *The Communion of Saints*, John Nava (born 1947), Cathedral of Our Lady of the Angels, Los Angeles, California, USA. © Cathedral of Our Lady of the Angels, Los Angeles, California, USA. Photo Frantisek Zvardon.

Pages 112-113: *Achtyrka, the Red Church*, Vassily Kandinsky (1866-1944), Russian Museum, Saint-Petersburg, Russia. © La Collection / Artothek. © Adagp, Paris 2009.

Pages 114-115: Cathedral of Our Lady of the Angels, Los Angeles, California, USA, José Rafael Moneo Vallés (born 1937) © Cathedral of Our Lady of the Angels, Los Angeles, California, USA.

Pages 116-117: *Mary and Elizabeth*, Dorothy Webster Hawksley (1884-1970), Private Collection. © The Maas Gallery, London, UK / Bridgeman Giraudon.

Pages 118-119: Interior of Notre-Dame-du-Haut Chapel, Ronchamp, France, Le Corbusier (1885-1965). © akg-images / L. M. Peter. © Adagp, Paris 2009.

Printed in October 2009
by Proost, Belgium
Edition number: MGN 09002

www.magnificat.com